# DON'T
# SHOOT!

## We may both be on the same side

## marvin phillips

COLLEGE PRESS PUBLISHING COMPANY
Box 1132, Joplin, MO 64802

Library of Congress Catalog Card Number: 90-80685
International Standard Book Number: 0-89900-352-4

Dedicated to
the elders
Garnett church of Christ
Tulsa, Okla.
where I have ministered for twenty years!

Ken Baldridge, Al Eagles, Eddie Hodge,
Willie Jackson and Bob Schweikhard

We stand together. Even when we do not agree!
And they back me in my feeble efforts
to faithfully preach the gospel
of Jesus Christ!

and

The Hillenburg Families
All members of the Garnett church
for the use of their lake house
where I have written
my last two books.
No one on earth supports me more faithfully
than these families!

# Table of Contents

# INTRODUCTION

I count it a high privilege to share in the message of this book. But more significantly in the life and work and fellowship of the author. An event in my life that will always be a treasured memory for me occurred in one of the *Soul Winning Workshops* in Tulsa, Oklahoma. College Press is glad to promote and attend this significant meeting. It just happened Marvin and I met just before he was scheduled to speak at one of the main sessions. He asked me in a most earnest manner: "Will you pray for me?" I of course said I would — it was not an unusual request — but Marvin grabbed my arm and said, *"Right now — right here!"* We stepped behind one of the display booths and knelt down together — I prayed for him — if there ever was an earnest request lifted to heaven it came from our hearts as we knelt together before our mutual Father — as we interceded through our mutual Intercessor. What happened there behind that display booth can and should happen throughout the more than 19,000 assemblies of our fellowship. Please, please read this book — do more than that. Commit yourself to strive in prayer for one another.

— Don DeWelt

## FOREWORD

There may be spiritual vultures perched on the fence waiting for such a book as this. They will pick my bones clean if it is possible. So, Marvin Phillips, why would you want to write a book on fellowship?

Surprisingly, the answer is simple. I love the church of God! I love the *whole* family of God. I want to stand strong for the truth. I want to oppose all error. Even in my own life! I don't know that I want to wound all the heels, but I know I want to help heal all the wounds.

Someone said, "If we keep doing the same old things in the same old ways, we'll keep on having the same old results!" Just take a look around. Churches of Christ aren't making the impact in the world we ought to be making. Add all the Restoration churches, and we are still an anonymous drop of gospel in an ocean of lostness. The world does not know we exist! Jesus said they'd believe if we became one!

Ours is the greatest plea in the world. But we've been incredibly successful in keeping it to ourselves. Step one, I think, is to regroup the forces. Then give a "certain sound" on the trumpet and God's army will go forth to battle. Together! Not against each other! To face a common foe!

I am committed to talking to anyone no matter what he believes. I've been in personal discussions with leaders of the Independent Christian churches, Discipling Movement and many branches of the non-instrumental churches of Christ. Truth has nothing of which to be afraid! I pen these words after much thought, study and prayer! My hope is to spawn greater desire to serve God, be loyal to His truth, love all His people and share the world's greatest message with a world that has lost its way!

DON'T SHOOT: WE MAY BOTH BE ON THE SAME SIDE!

# 1

## *LOVE AMONG THE SPLINTERS!*

Can you hear Him praying? Is that sweat? It looks more like blood. He's about to go to the cross. The most agonizing death anyone has ever known. That's the extent He would go to save us. And He's praying. Not for Himself. He's praying for us. "Oh, Father. That they all may be one. All those who believe on Me, that they might be one. The world won't believe I AM Who I say I AM, if they're not one. Let them be united as You and I are united. One spirit. One love. One cause. My last prayer. My dying wish. Please, let them be one!"

What a prayer! The entire seventeenth chapter of John is the prayer Jesus prayed right before Calvary. He spoke of that which was closest to Him. He spoke of us. Of the "blood bought ones." And He wanted us one. United!

And how have we answered that prayer? Yes, I'm talking to those of us in what we like to call the Restoration Movement. The very words call for making things like they were; like Jesus wanted them. Jesus wanted what He wrote, and He wrote what He wanted. He wanted His gospel, His church. He wanted the world led from sin to salvation in His marvelous Family, the church of Jesus Christ. And He bought that church with His blood.

We've talked more about religious unity than any group on earth. But we have also divided about as much as any. There are three major branches from what was known as the Restoration Movement in America: the Disciples of Christ, the churches of Christ, and the Independent Christian church.

And then let's talk about unity among the "regulars." That comes from the difference between "innocent pleasure" and "sinful pleasure." Sinful pleasure is what *you* do; innocent pleasure is what I do! Got the picture?

Anyway, how are things among the non-instrumentals? We have often heard the plea, "leave your denominational creeds and practices and unite with *us* on the Word of God." Unite with *which one* of us? Our own directory, "Where the Saints Meet!" lists fifteen kinds of us. No, as of 1988 there are sixteen kinds of us. The codes list OC (one cup), NC (non-class), NI (Non-institutional). The latest designation is ME. Are you ready for this? This designation is given churches of Christ who choose to place a sign on their property that reads,

"WHITE CITY CHURCH
. . . a church of Christ serving White City."

Now get the picture. There is no mention of a church building in the Bible; no mention of a sign, and no instructions for what to put on a sign if we had one. Yet some question the "faithfulness" of a church if their sign does not read *"Church of Christ."* We have truly shattered the cross of Christ.

*MARVIN PHILLIPS: PRE-1960!*

I was raised to believe my branch of the churches of Christ

12

(non-instrumentals) was the only true church. I viewed the Christian churches as "all alike." I did not know the difference in Disciples churches and Independent Christian churches. I felt they had no regard for Bible authority and all had women preachers. I had heard reports of barefooted dancing girls doing interpretive dancing of "My Faith Looks Up to Thee" in the worship services, and was properly appalled. I heard they accepted anyone's baptism whether immersion or sprinkling, adult or infant. I wanted no part of them!

My view of the "anti's" was similar. Some were anti-class, some were anti-communion cup. Others were anti (against) such things as orphan homes, located preachers and a host of other things. As a small boy, I remember my dad preaching in a little "one cup" church in Verdi, Texas. At least they were one cup until old brother Jenkins developed tuberculosis. They suddenly became a "two cup" church. I asked about it, and never got a clear answer. I viewed all these churches as "lost" and thought they viewed us as lost!

I was raised to debate. As a young preacher I began debating denominational preachers. And I was good at it. I wanted to be a champion debater among churches of Christ. I wanted to nail hide after hide of denominational preachers to the barn door. I thought this would make me a good soldier of Jesus Christ. I considered all denominational preachers as enemies of truth. And I could not carry on a decent conversation with any of them without turning it into an argument!


## 1960: SILOAM SPRINGS, ARKANSAS

When anyone looks back over his life, he will see certain years or events as "turning points." The year I moved my family to Siloam Springs was such a year. I had held meetings for them for the past couple of years. One night the Christian church preacher was in the audience. That used to mean, "sic 'em!'' Members would come inform you a denominational preacher was there, and you were expected to make it hot for him. Well, as he approached me at the door after my sermon he said, "Good sermon. I brought some of my people with me. I like to expose them to good gospel preaching!" To say I was nonplussed is an understatement. He meant it!

I went home (Port Lavaca, Texas) and he kept preaching along the lines of what a New Testament church ought to be. They fired him. And the church split. The resulting new church rented a building at the edge of town and advertised under the name "Christ's Church."

Well the church of Christ preacher also moved from Siloam Springs, leaving both churches without a preacher. Both churches went after their "champions." The Christian church hired the man who had been preaching in their last few meetings. "Christ's Church" hired a man, and the church of Christ called me to come. We all hit town gunning for one another. Before long we were having regular weekly Bible studies with the "Christ's Church" group. We boldly looked at our differences, and tried to convince each other we were right. The difficult part was praying. I had never called on anyone outside the church of Christ to lead prayer. But now here we were, trying to study together. So various ones led prayer. It was a good old time.

Then we hit a snag. The "Christ's Church" group invited me to a fellowship dinner they were having, and asked that I preach to their group. They further asked that I preach on why we do not use instrumental music in worship. In fear and trembling I went. Had I known then that I would be criticized many times over in the next decade of my life for such things, I might never have gone. Isn't it amazing how afraid of each other we are? I have since pled, "Judge me by *what* I say; not *where* I say it!"

Well to make a long story short, these two groups felt like instrumental music was too little an issue to keep us apart. We joined together, without the instrument, and had a marvelous time serving God for the next two years of my ministry there.

But I must tell you a most marvelous experience that resulted from that union. Someone began to question whether these folks from the Christian church had been baptized right. We argued that there was no such thing as church of Christ baptism; only Bible baptism. But the problem persisted. So I took the problem to my associate preacher (upon the merger, they had kept both preachers). It was decided I should preach a sermon on "Bible Baptism," and everyone would take a serious look to see if they had obeyed this command of God.

The invitation was sung. And would you believe? Down the aisle came four people to be baptized. One from the Christian church to say his baptism had not been according to the Bible. One of our own deacon's wives also requested that she be rebaptized upon really examining the scriptures. The other was an elderly couple that both of us preachers had been studying with. They said simply, "You were both coming to our house to study with us. You were both showing us the same verses and urging us to do the same thing. But you were in different churches. We felt whichever way we went, one of you would be unhappy. How wonderful it is, now that you are united, that we can just obey the Lord, and worship together."

## 1962-1970: AUSTRALIA

My family moved again in 1962. This time to Perth, Western Australia. It was our desire and opportunity to join the Rudy Wyatt and Ron Durham families who had preceded us there by a year. Perth was a large city of 400,000 population. We selected a large section of that city where there was no church of any kind. Before long we became aware that there was a group in town called the "Associated Churches of Christ." We soon found out they were the counterparts of the Christian church in the United States. They looked to America for leadership, but as yet had not figured out whether they belonged to the Disciples or the Independent churches. There was great struggle among them even on subjects as basic as baptism for the remission of sins. We met their leaders and had several good "forum type" discussions where both sides were presented, and questions were asked from the floor. I learned valuable lessons on how brethren could get together to discuss their differences without a debate format or the necessity of excessive quarreling. This would be my background for the later Restoration Forums that would follow in America. I learned to listen more and reason more rationally. We saw several preachers and members change. But the main thing was that we were becoming less argumentative. And the church where I preached was becoming more of a "family" like the Bible portrays God's people! That word "family" would shape my thinking and direction for the future. It would invade all my study, thought, and examinations with others with whom I differed.

## TULSA, OKLAHOMA: 1970-

After two tours in Australia, my family moved to Tulsa, Oklahoma, in May of 1970. We began working with a newly established church (East Tulsa, now known as Garnett church of Christ). It began with 91 charter members. It has grown to over 1600 members at present.

It was a loving, growing, evangelistic church from the start. The word "family" came up again. We just began referring to the church as "family." We thanked people for visiting with the "family of God" today. We welcomed baptized believers into the "family." We even named our bulletin "The Family of God." It began to have an effect on the people. We had talked so much about family, they began acting like one. It showed up in fellowship. Members began treating one another with a deeper love and appreciation. It permeated every aspect of church life. When folks began asking me to explain the phenomena of church life and growth, we soon began to realize it was our recognition that we were indeed the Family of God!

Getting that "family feeling" will have an effect on the local congregation. It will affect how you feel about sister churches. And it most assuredly will affect your thinking on the whole Restoration Movement. When it really dawns on us that we are family we will treat each other far better than we do now!

Some time in 1970 I met Manny Loveall. Manny was a printer by trade, and the minister for the Town and Country Christian church. Before long we were good friends. One thing led to another. We thought we ought to get the two groups of preachers together for some discussions of our differences to see if some solutions might be found, and more fellowship enjoyed.

Preachers from both sides met in lunch meetings on three different occasions. Manny and I both spoke the first time at the "ice-breaker," on "Love Among the Splinters." There was brisk discussion and questions. We planned the second meeting. It was on "Bible Authority and the Silence of the Scripture," and followed the same format. The third discussion was on "Worship," and things went downhill from there.

Most of the non-instrumental brethren figured we weren't going to convince them on the "Instrument Question" and felt the talks were best abandoned. And that's what happened. Back in neutral corners. Suspicious. No fellowship. Divided!

## JOPLIN, MISSOURI: 1984

I was restless about not talking to my brothers in the Christian church. I stumbled across the passionate spirit of Don DeWelt who shared the same unrest. Don was a Professor in

17

Ozark Bible College (since changed to Ozark Christian College). He runs College Press, and has a determined spirit that we ought to try much harder than we've ever tried before to see what fellowship might be discovered so that God's people might work together for the answer to our Lord's prayer for unity, and the salvation of the lost of the world. Don had been in correspondence with Alan Cloyd (of Restoration Ministry). Together they planned the first Restoration Forum in Joplin, on the campus of O.C.C. in 1984.

There was an air of difference about this meeting that could not be mistaken. Representative brethren from both sides came together, but without a divisive spirit. They shared openly and honestly. They discussed differences and offered solutions. The format was good. One speaker from each side would speak on the same subject. Then we would adjourn to smaller discussion groups, pre-assigned to put 5 of one side with 5 of the other side. They would discuss the speeches just heard. Then we would come back together and reporters would share what went on in each group. Then on to the next speech. There was not a hint of compromise. We ate together. We prayed together. And most important of all, we made plans to talk again. At this writing, there have been seven of these Restoration Forums (Joplin, Tulsa, Pepperdine, Milligan College, two in Ohio, and Lincoln, Ill.). Brethren are refusing to give up. That (or maybe I should say "He") which holds us together is stronger than that which keeps us apart. At least, we are coming to understand each other better. At best, we will discover ways to work together where we do not have differences.

## *BROTHERHOOD CRITICISM!*

To be sure, there has been a lot of criticism surrounding these talks. Mostly, I have to say, it has been on rumors that are not founded in fact. It has been charged that some of us are try-

18

ing to "merge" the two churches together. We've been charged with "selling out the Restoration Movement." It was erroneously reported that there had been an agreement at these meetings not to mention the issue of instrumental music. All these charges are untrue. The music question has been a vital part of every forum, complete with the finest debate on instrumental music you are likely to hear in your life. The place was Cincinnati. The year was 1987. The participants were Don DeWelt and Rubel Shelly. Both men did a tremendous job defending their various positions and calling for unity based on what they believed the Bible taught!

## FUTURE OF THE RESTORATION FORUMS!

One thing is for sure. Restoration Forums are here to stay. Too many brethren are too excited about getting together in this honest, open setting. They are open to all comers. I would urge any of you with skepticism to make a trip to one of them. You'll be glad you did!

And what's going to happen? Will the instrument question ever be resolved? Some brethren believe it is simple· "Just give up the instrument and we can be united!" But this is precisely what the anti-class and the one cup brethren have been pleading with us for years. It seems we only want to apply this logic when it suits "us!"

Sadly, I predict it won't! It takes its place right beside the divorce and remarriage question. It is serious, and we must talk about it. But in either case, we're going to need to stand before God so He can at last straighten us out. In the meantime we can keep loving, keep studying, and keep praying. Above all else, we've got to keep the lines of communication open. We claim we love the Father. Maybe just to prove it we'll stop beating up on His kids!

# 2

## THE MINISTRY OF RECONCILIATION!

So from now on we regard no one from a worldly point of view. Though we once regarded Christ in this way, we do so no longer. Therefore if anyone is in Christ, he is a new creation; the old has gone, the new has come. All this is from God, who reconciled us to himself through Christ and gave us the ministry of reconciliation: that God was reconciling the world to himself in Christ, not counting men's sins against them. And he has committed to us the message of reconciliation. We are therefore Christ's ambassadors, as though God were making his appeal through us. We implore you on Christ's behalf: Be reconciled to God. (II Cor. 5:16-20)

You might want to take off your shoes. For this ground (these verses we've just read) is holy ground. This is the mission of the church. We are urged in the fear of the Lord (v. 11). The love of Christ compels us (v. 14). We are to quit regarding people from a worldly point of view (v. 16). The words "reconciled" and "reconciliation" are mentioned five times in the above passage.

*This* is the mission of the church! Let everything we do be done for that purpose. Our world was recently shocked when accusation of scandal was pointed at Oral Roberts, Jim and Tammy Bakker, and Jimmy Swaggart. These things are nothing new. Take another look at II Samuel, chapter twelve. God's man, David, had been caught in such a scandal. And he was guilty! Of the whole list. Lust! Adultery! Murder! And finally, "cover up"! We will not forget the courageous Nathan whom God sent! His fearless sermon left David dangling on the ropes as Nathan pointed that finger saying, "You are the man!" But Nathan was not sent to condemn David, but to reconcile him to God. And his ministry of reconciliation worked. Because of David's right attitude toward sin and repentance, he was able to stay king, marry Bathsheba, raise Solomon and rule Israel for forty years. God said in the Old Testament, and repeated it in the New, "I have found a man (David) after my own heart!" That's what reconciliation is all about.

Our job is not just to point out all the errors in the world. There's too much division and alienation in our world. Russia and the United States are at odds with each other. Iraq and Iran shoot at each other. And in the name of religion (?) fighting goes on in Ireland, Israel and Syria. On the home front homes are divided by divorce. Churches fight and divide. The church is to be the agency of reconciliation in times like these.

For he himself is our peace, who has made the two one and has destroyed the barrier, the dividing wall of hostility, by abolishing in his flesh the law with its commandments and regulations. His purpose was to create in himself one new man out of the two thus making peace, and in this new body to reconcile both of them to God through the cross, by which he put to death their hostility. He came and preached peace to you who were far away and peace to those who were near. For through him we both have access to the Father by one spirit. (Eph. 2:14-18)

22

## AREAS THAT NEED RECONCILIATION!

*Enemies.* In the sermon on the mount, Jesus taught, "You have heard that it was said, love your neighbor and hate your enemy. But I tell you: love your enemies and pray for those who persecute you" (Matt. 5:43,44). And again, "Do not repay anyone evil for evil. Be careful to do what is right in the eyes of everybody. Do not take revenge, my friends, but leave room for God's wrath, for it is written, 'It is mine to avenge; I will repay,' says the Lord. On the contrary: if your enemy is hungry, feed him; if he is thirsty, give him something to drink. In doing this you will heap burning coals on his head. Do not be overcome by evil, but overcome evil with good" (Rom. 12:17-21).

If you've got an enemy, God wants you to practice reconciliation. There are simply too many folks who don't get along. They carry grudges for years. They fuss and fight. They refuse to speak to one another. And God says "I've given you the message and the ministry of reconciliation. Let's turn those enemies into friends in the name of Jesus.

*Marriages.* Aye, there's the rub. Too many marriages are going down the tube. And in the Bible belt of America some 50% of our marriages end in divorce. In Florida the rate is 67%. And some have suggested that as high as 83% of our marriages are failures in terms of love, unity and commitment!

But it doesn't have to be this way. God ordained on the first page of the Bible that man was to "leave" and "cleave"! Leave father and mother was defined as relationship. Husbands and wives are to be Number One in each other's lives. No other relationship on earth is to be as important as that one. And then there's "cleaving." Leave and cleave! They are to cling to each other. Physically? Yes, but more importantly they are to be an emotional and spiritual strength to one another. They are to be each other's best cheer leader.

Jesus said, "Therefore what God has joined together, let man not separate" (Matt. 19:6). This is a great area where the ministry of reconciliation is to take place. We've got to train our people to be "solution conscious" rather than "problem conscious." There are no unsolvable problems. Only people who refuse to solve them in the name of Jesus.

*Denominationalism.* Jesus never intended His people to be divided religiously. In that great prayer in John chapter seventeen Jesus prayed, "that all of them may be one, Father, just as you are in me and I am in you." But while we've preached against religious division, we have been derelict in talking to those with whom we differ. It seems easier to condemn them than to work on reconciliation. We've talked about them when we should have been talking "to them"!

*The Restoration Movement.* The aim of the restoration movement was two-fold; to restore Christianity to its first century purity, and to call all believers into fellowship in one body. The message was "Restoration." One does not read the modern day phenomenon of "one church withdrawing fellowship from another church." It simply isn't there!

And we have largely missed the message of Romans 16:17 which says,

> I urge you brothers, to watch out for those who cause divisions and put obstacles in your way that are contrary to the teaching you have learned. Keep away from them!

We have interpreted this verse to teach "mark, withdraw from and avoid anyone who disagrees with you!" I insist it doesn't teach this at all. It rather warns against those who "cause division." It is argued by some that "they" cause division by differing with us, or practicing something we do not believe. Brethren, there are many differences in the church of Christ today over which people do not divide. The sin here is of "causing division," being divisive, building walls where God has not built them. Let a man think long and prayerfully before he does anything that splits asunder the body of Christ.

A fresh dose of Romans, chapters fourteen and fifteen are in order here. There we are admonished to "accept those whose faith is weak," "don't judge another man's servant," "one man esteems every day alike; another man esteems one day above another, *each one should be fully convinced in his own mind*," "accept one another then, just as Christ accepted you, in order to bring praise to God."

Paul could have marked the church at Corinth. While he spoke plainly about their sins, he refused to mark them, and urge "faithful brethren" to worship elsewhere. John could have similarly marked five of the seven churches of Asia. But he did not. We've got to quit filing "separate maintenance" on each other. We are *one family*. Have we forgotten that?

*Then there's reconciliation within the local church.* That's really the subject when Paul declares, "let there be no divisions among you" (I Cor. 1:10). It is a local church of which he is speaking. Again, "Get rid of all bitterness, rage and anger, brawling and slander, along with every form of malice. Be kind and compassionate to one another, forgiving each other, just as in Christ God forgave you" (Eph 4:31,32). Listen to this warning penned in Galatians 5:15, "If you keep on biting and devouring each other, watch out or you will be destroyed by each other"! If ever words fit our present situation it is these words. In heaven's name, dear brethren, cease this hostility. Jesus told us how we'd be recognized as His people. And it wasn't by our sign out front, that we take the Lord's supper every Sunday, or even if we baptize for the remission of sins. These are all important. But hear his words, "*all men will know that you are my disciples if you love one another*" (John 13:35).

*And then let's practice reconciliation brother-to-brother!* Jesus said, "Therefore, if you are offering your gift at the altar and there remember that your brother has something against you, leave your gift there in front of the altar. First go and be reconciled to your brother; then come and offer your gift" (Matt. 5:23).

25

It is so important that we stay in covenant relationship with God. But it is equally important that we stay in loving unity with each other. Worship is important. But God here directs us to get right with each other so that our worship to God might not be hindered.

## THE GREATEST AREA OF "RECONCILIATION"!

Finally there is evangelism. The real mission of the church. The single reason Jesus left heaven and came to earth. "For the Son of Man came to seek and to save what was lost" (Luke 19:10). Soul winning is all there is! The *big* problem in the world today is *sin*. And you've noticed in the word sin, "I" is right in the middle of it! Isaiah said,

> Surely the arm of the Lord is not too short to save nor his ear too dull to hear. But your iniquities have separated you from your God; your sins have hidden his face from you, so that he will not hear! (Isa. 59:1,2)

Therefore we have the ministry of reconciliation. We need the passion of an apostle Paul who said, "I have become all things to all men so that by all possible means I might save some" (I Cor. 9:22). Churches need to be involved in soul winning. Too many of us major in minors. We need to major in soul winning. We need to consider soul winning the most important work in the world. Bringing people into a saving relationship with Jesus Christ is more important than all the "issues" that divide us. Jesus made us fishers of men. But some would rather fight than fish!

I've noticed that soul winners don't fight. If brethren who differ over some issue know that they are both committed to winning people to Jesus, they will find a way to get along. They may differ clearly and seriously. But they will find a way to stay

26

together as they help each other save the lost from a devil's hell! It's the old adage again: "the old mule can't pull while he's kicking. And he can't kick while he's pulling"! When our churches get serious about soul winning we'll work out a way to have fellowship with each other. Show me our greatest champions of division, holding brother from brother, and I'll show you a man whose life is devoid of personal evangelism. It would be interesting to find out, wouldn't it!?

Brethren, we've been given the ministry of reconciliation. Not one of arguing, but of settling arguments. Not dividing, but uniting. Not damning but saving. Not content till all are back with God, safe in the fold, on their way to heaven.

A submarine went down in World War II. It wasn't far from shore and the Navy had their frog men on the job to find the sub before its oxygen supply ran out. The first man to reach the sub found it lying in darkness on the bottom of the harbor. He tapped in morse code on the hull of the ship, "Are you there?" The urgent reply came, "Yes, we are here!" He tapped next, "Help is on the way!" And from within came the frantic question, "How long will it be?"

Christian friends the ship is in the water. The world is in sin and time is running out. And as I look here and there at Christians and churches urgently trying to become what God wants them to be, I know that help is on the way. But the urgent question of the day, as it was for that submarine, "How long will it be?"

# 3

## THE RESTORATION MOVEMENT FOR TODAY AS I SEE IT!

*This chapter is taken from an address at the 1987 Restoration Forum.*

Then God said to Jacob, 'Go up to Bethel and settle there, and build an altar there to God who appeared to you when you were fleeing from your brother Esau.' So Jacob said to his household and to all who were with him, 'Get rid of the foreign gods you have with you and purify yourselves and change your clothes. Then come, let us go up to Bethel, where I will build an altar to God, who answered me in the day of my distress and who has been with me wherever I have gone.' So they gave Jacob all the foreign gods they had and the rings in their ears, and Jacob buried them under the oak at Shechem. Then they set out, and the terror of God fell upon the towns all around them so that no one pursued them. (Gen. 35:1-5)

Our lesson text is a great story. It makes great peraching! But it also has some special lessons and applications for the Restoration Movement today.

Jacob once had a great relationship with God, but he lost it. He found he could get it back, and did what was necessary to do so. He paid the price for restoration, and the end result was that "the terror of God fell upon the towns all around them" (vs. 5).

I believe the people of God once had it good! It was good on Pentecost (Acts 2), when the Holy Spirit came, the gospel was preached and the church of our Lord began. It was good during the last century when such men as Alexander Campbell, Walter Scott and others were calling for an end to denominationalism, and a return to simple New Testament Christianity!

But somewhere along the way, we lost it! That marvelous plea, so needed in every age, turned to "in-fighting" among ourselves. We who preach unity more than anyone else on earth, are some of the most divided people in the world today! Sound doctrine is not always to blame! Sometimes it is just our own stubbornness, or refusal to make honest, though sometimes painful, efforts to "keep the unity of the Spirit through the bond of peace."

So Jacob lost it. And we can lose it today! But, praise God, He knew he could get it back. Just look at what he had to do. He had to:

(1) Decide to go back!
(2) Get rid of the hindrances!
(3) Purify himself!
(4) Change his clothes!
(5) Make the trip!

But when the decision was made, and the price was paid, the Bible records, "and the terror of God fell upon the towns around them so that no one pursued them"!

Oh, I would love to see us so united, so right with God, such a wonderful force in our world today, that no one dare oppose the people of God! Yea, in fact, who would want to?

30

## APPLICATIONS FOR US TODAY!

We've got to make a decision! We usually get what we want more than anything else. If we decide to go back to God, back to unity, we'll find a way, with God's help to do it!

Then we'll have to get rid of the hindrances. That is, anything that stands between us and God. It will be time for a hard look at the Book of God. It is serious enough that there are differences among us. It will be more so, if any among us are not in dead earnest about the need for Scripture backing everything we do!

Thirdly, we need to purify ourselves. We need to be willing to clean up our own backyards; to repent of our own sinfulness. And we need more willingness to apologize for actions and attitudes that are anything but "Christ-like"! We've been too quick to point the finger of blame, without seeing the three fingers pointing right back at ourselves!

And we need to "change clothes"! Of course we must not abandon God, His Book, nor even our convictions. But we need to look more like Jesus in what we do! At baptism we were "clothed with Christ" (Gal. 3:27). Much of what we do to, and about each other, doesn't look much like Jesus!

And then the power of God came! When God's people are right with God, and with each other, there is simply nothing on earth they cannot accomplish. We need that Restoration today!


## THE PLAN OF JESUS WAS AN ETERNAL PLAN!

Salvation through the gospel and the church was in the "eternal purpose of God" (Eph. 3:10,11). The plan was renewed again in Gethsemane, where Jesus prayed for His followers to be one, stating that the whole world would believe "when his people were one" (John 17:21). The "essentials" of that plan were laid down in Ephesians 4, namely "One body, Spirit,

31

hope, Lord, faith, baptism and God" (vv. 4-6).

That plan was thwarted by a lot of things. False teachers (Rom. 16:17) and "wolves" among leadership (Acts 20:29) played a part in leading the church into apostasy. But Jesus meant for that plan and that church to spread throughout the whole world! It was, and is, the most serious charge ever given!

## ANOTHER LOOK AT THE "PLEA"!

Is the plea valid? Does Jesus have a right to have His church exist in the world? Does He have a say in what it preaches, how its people act, and who gets a chance to belong to His family? Surely we believe what Jesus did on His "earth trip," and what He prayed to the Father, has a right to exist as long as the world stands!

Well, exactly what is the plea? Is it "sameness"? When the scripture says, "all of you agree with one another" (I Cor. 1:10), does it really mean "in everything"? Are there no areas where we can disagree and still be the people of God? Are honest, truth seeking men doomed to isolation and division if they come to different conclusions on an issue? If sincere, God-fearing men have strong differences about Bible classes, orphan homes, or instrumental music in worship, is there no way they can still be the "Family of God," and keep loving each other, discussing their differences and staying together in the Family?

Some demands for "sameness" are sound, sane and sensible! In my search for the "essentials," I have come up with six:

(1) The Being and Position of God.

(2) The Lordship of Jesus.

(3) The inspiration and authority of Scripture.

(4) The glory and importance of the church.

(5) The new birth.

(6) Genuine commitment to the Will, Way and Word of God.

How can anything else be "essential"? And "genuine commitment" shuts off any loophole of someone who just "doesn't care what the Bible says; I'll do it my own way"! It allows for honest error of the one totally committed to God and His Word. It seems to me if this is not allowed, we are all in trouble.

## A LOOK AT "US"

Nineteen centuries this side of the establishment of the church should find the people of God making progress on internal unity, and external evangelism. The world is supposed to be "seeing our good works, and glorifying the Father" (Matt. 5:16). Is that the world's picture of "us"?

The "Restoration Movement" itself has at least three branches. In my view, the gap is widening between the Disciples and Independents. The Independents are plagued by tendencies toward liberalism. And the "non-instrumentals" are split about sixteen ways!

Dare anyone look at this pitiful scene and say, "That's the way it's supposed to be!"? Can we really honor Jesus by maintaining isolation from each other? We are better at talking "about" each other, than talking "to" each other! It's time to risk the critics and do something that sounds more like Jesus and His precious Word!

## WELL, WHAT DO WE DO ABOUT OUR DIFFERENCES?

First of all, I suggest that we recognize and admit each other's genuine efforts to be "scriptural." Our doctrinal differences are mostly "hermeneutical" anyway! And whose hermeneutic is right? I really believe mine is the best! But I honestly confess to you that there is weakness in both our approaches to Bible authority! One has weaknesses toward

33

liberalism. The other has weaknesses toward fractionalism. Why can't we see this, admit it, and respect each other? There are an equal number of men on both sides who passionately want to be pleasing to God and interpret His Word accurately.

Secondly, let us discuss our serious differences regularly, openly and fearlessly. These Forums are healthy and necessary! When men can't rationally discuss issues, it evidences fear and possibly insecurity. Could it be that the more vehement among us are really unsure of their own convictions or standing with God? I've noticed the older I get, and the more sure I am of what I believe, I have less fear in sharing with others. I am certain I have things to teach others. I am equally certain I have much to learn. Bring on truth!

Thirdly, do not violate your convictions. In all this "Restoration Forum" talk, no one is asked to violate his convictions! No one is being asked to "go along" with a practice he feels violates the Word of God! But get all the fellowship you can get! Just because you disagree over one thing, don't build walls of division between the children of God. Refuse to have fellowship with anything you feel is wrong, but don't isolate from God's children and pretend they are not even in the Family!

## HOPE FOR THE FUTURE

I am optimistic as I stand before you today! I believe great strides are being made in the unity for which Christ died. I am aware that just "standing here" in a situation like this would have been unthought of just a few years ago. Now, good brothers like Don DeWelt, Alan Cloyd, Reuel Lemmons, Rubel Shelly and others have decided "something must be done." They have pioneered the way. To be sure, some are fearful. They mainly misunderstand what is being done. They are afraid, some of us are going to "sell them out." That's kind of laughable. For how could anyone of us standing here make any other brother do anything wrong? We can hardly coerce them into doing what is plainly written in God's truth. Our brethren are a hardy lot. We've taught them to "search the scriptures"; we've warned them against apostasy enough. It isn't likely that "truth" will ever divide "truth seekers"!

But we must lose our fear of the "hit men" in the brotherhood. Some of the loudest criticism of "unity talks" come from men who have never built a church, don't have a better plan, and content themselves with shooting down any plan anyone else has. It is time to get this in perspective and move on. We have been more afraid of each other than of God. It is time for that to change!

We must get out of "judgmentalism" and "isolationism"! Because of past ignorance we don't really know who each other is. Let's talk. Let's listen to one another. We need each other. These forums, and any other format that puts us thinking, praying, talking and studying together, has got to be a good thing. I'm for more of it.

Last of all, let's keep preaching the Book. We are by heritage and by necessity, a people who believe in Bible authority. We are a "thus saith the Lord" people. To whatever extent our pulpits have abandoned this, let's get it back. God wrote what He wanted and wanted what He wrote. "My way" will never improve on the Word of God!

## CONCLUSION

A hurting world needs the restoration gospel today! What was preached by Jesus and His apostles is still needed today — complete and without alteration. Our squabbling shuts them out. They can't hear us for seeing us. Our divisions shackle the cross. Our arrogance shames the bleeding Jesus. Our civil wars mortally wound the body of Christ.

Someone has to stand up and say "enough!" "No more!"

Someone has to break free from the intimidation of men. We must get tied to Jesus and the Bible. We must get free from brotherhood politics, papers and demands from self-appointed Popes! Let's be right (with God); be nice (to those without and within); and then be fearless!

I want Jesus to be proud of what I do and what I stand for. I hope the rest of you love me and are proud of me, too.

But that's not what counts.

# 4

## PRECIOUS PEOPLE I HAVE LOVED AMONG MY INSTRUMENTAL BRETHREN!

*This chapter is from an address at the 1988 Restoration Forum.*

My first knowledge of the Independent Christian churches was in 1960 in Siloam Springs, Arkansas. I was preaching there in a gospel meeting. The local Christian church preacher came out to hear me preach. Shortly after the meeting he was fired. I've always hoped I was not to blame. Anyway the church split. The third church was called simply, "Christ's Church!" Also the Church of Christ preacher left. So both churches hired the preachers they'd been using in meetings. Christ's Church hired Charles Gillespie. We all hit town gunning for one another.

But it wasn't long before we began a weekly study and prayer session with Christ's Church! They eventually asked me to preach for their monthly fellowship luncheon.

Needless to say I was reluctant. They asked that I preach to them about why we don't use instrumental music.

Further study and association together, and they were considering merging with us. But as one of their members said, "We like what you say, but how do we really know you are a New Testament church?" It seemed Biblical to say, "come and see!" They did! For six months they visited with us. Then one lively June Sunday morning they all came forward during the invitation song, and the two churches became one! It was marvelous to find that indeed "We are brethren!"

## WHO ARE THESE PEOPLE?

In 1984 we had that historic first Restoration Forum in Joplin, on the campus of Ozark Bible College (since called Ozark Christian College). The discussions were open and great. But all could tell there was a reluctance on the part of many non-instrumental brethren. We had simply equated you with the Disciples of Christ. We imagined you baptized babies, had women elders and cared nothing about Bible authority! So after a quick huddle by the "fiddlers," a fine brother gave a comprehensive speech identifying the Independent churches, and their difference to the Disciples. It was like a bolt out of the blue for many to find, as one non-instrumental brother put it, "I've learned today I have about a million brothers and sisters I didn't know I had!"

Now it isn't that we don't have some serious and troublesome problems between us. Some of these don't affect our corporate worship; others do! But along this beautiful, challenging, exciting road of exploring what God's book really does teach, and pursuing all the possiblities of fellowship among us, I've met some great men in the instrumental fellowship whom I really love.

38

Among them, my illustrious co-speaker here this afternoon, *Don DeWelt*. How do you *not* love Don DeWelt? With that wonderful spirit and that contagious smile? It's as if he's up to something! Don has a deep love for the book of Christ, the cause of Christ and the Church of Christ.

He's my brother! And not because I've decided to "brother" him. It's because he was born into the Family of God the same way I was. He was added to the church by the same Lord. We're in the same Family. And he's trying to do and be the same thing I'm trying to do and be! And Don makes a lot of mistakes. He's wrong about a lot of things. He's wrong nearly as many times as I am.

I love him for those great books he has written that have blessed so many lives. *If You Want to Preach. Acts Made Actual.* I've taught both of these to men aspiring to do great things for God. His *Romans Realized* is as good a commentary as you'll find on that marvelous book.

Then there's *One Body*! It took a Don DeWelt to think up that marvelous idea to start a publication, where brethren on all sides of the fence could write and present their point of view about unity and fellowship. And trust Don to want to take it further to present to every denominational preacher in America the marvelous Restoration Plea.

Don and I have corresponded back and forth, studied and prayed together, and spoken on the same platform. College Press has asked to publish a book from me. And I am honored to be asked and will get to it as soon as I can. We may disagree on a few things, but I know if Don DeWelt and I found ourselves together in the same town, we would find a way to worship God together. I'm happy to count him my brother in Christ.

*Manny Loveall* was a printer by trade, and part time preacher. He's the first instrumental brother I really got to know after moving to Tulsa in 1970. Forming a fast friendship, Manny and I arranged early discussions between our brethren in the Tulsa area. I remember I spoke on "Love Among the Splinters." Our association was not long, but it was good! I admire a spirit that says, "We're in the same Family. I've got to know you better. Is there a problem between us? If there is, let's work to fix it!"

We preach unity more than any religious group on earth; and practice division about as much as any. We'd have better luck nailing jello to the side of a tree than to get some brethren to agree to just sit down and talk. Manny was an exception!

*Marshall Leggett* is President of Milligan College. He's another brother I love and admire very much. We've corresponded together, talked and prayed together. I've been on the campus of Milligan several times for the School of Ministry. Marshall and I both participated in the Brush Run Revival a few years ago. I preached on that old outdoor platform next to the foundation of the first church Alexander Campbell built in America. Marshall does an excellent job portraying the early Restorers in full costume. He did Thomas Campbell and Barton W. Stone the two nights we were together. That would be a great presentation in any church. No one knows Restoration History better than Marshall Leggett. He has a passion for Bible authority, fellowship and evangelism. I recommend his great book on *The Restoration Ideal*. His treatment on *The Acapella Brethren* is extremely charitable! From such men as Marshall Leggett you simply cannot divide. You hang in there. You keep studying and praying together. And in the meantime, you get all the fellowship you can without violating your convictions.

And then there's *Ken Idleman*. Ken is the young and dynamic President of Ozark Christian College in Joplin, Missouri. I've stayed in his home. And never been treated finer. I've spoken on the campus of OCC to a large and appreciative audience. They have the same problems the rest of us have. They lost some support just because I preached in that pulpit. Ken is a great preacher and a great administrator. He did a fine job as a speaker on Restoration Forum II, which we hosted in Tulsa. I want to do more with Ken Idleman and Ozark Christian College.

*Victor Knowles* was my "Co-Respondent" in Restoration V held in Cincinnati last year. We both had the same subject, "The Restoration Movement for Today as I see it!" Victor spoke first. All I could do was give him a resounding "Amen!" It was terrific. And I got a standing ovation from both sides for my own speech of the night. It just shows how much we have in common, and how the love can grow, when you give it a chance.

I've enjoyed being on "Restoration Panels" with Victor. It's always going to be enjoyable with a man of his spirit.

Victor does a magnificent job as editor of *One Body*! I've enjoyed his articles and editorials. I preached his "God Save the World" as the final night keynote speech of the Tulsa International Workshop last March. I didn't tell anyone it was Victor's speech. It was a great speech. I wanted them to think I was that smart!

"And what more shall I say?" (shades of Heb. 11:32). For time would fail me to tell of such men as Roy Blackmore, Bill Campbell, Harold McCracken, B.A. Austin and Glen Liston, all from the Tulsa area. Men I eat lunch with once a month. Men I love in the Lord. There's Gary Washburn with whom I enjoyed a closeness till he moved from Cleveland, Oklahoma, to Auburn, Michigan. I've since preached up there in a joint-fellowship spiritual enrichment weekend! And Bill Pile, from out in California. Great spirit! Great man!

And finally I want to salute, and express my love to the "Master's Men" as they are affectionately called on the campus of Kentucky Christian College, Grayson, Ky. I teach in that course one week each September. That program was a marvelous idea. I get those forty or so preachers about two years out of Bible college. They learned the Book; then they hit the brethren. Most of them are down. I get to boost them and talk to them about God, growth and glory. My newest book, *The JOY Factor of Church Growth* is the material from that course. And the book is dedicated to the "Seventy-five men who sat at my feet while I taught this material and went out to put it into practice." Among those fine young men, Lynn Camp, Jerry Thompson, Tom Burgess and Wayne Manning stand out.

Here is our future as I see it. Let's recognize the "whole family of God." Let's recognize the fact that the Independent Christian churches and non-instrumental churches of Christ have more in common than any two other segments in the Restoration Movement. A recent published survey of this quoted our "issues agreement" at 85%. Let's build on that! Let's continue to discuss differences that hinder fellowship. Let's learn to seriously disagree without drawing lines of fellowship between us. Let's love the Father and to prove we do let's love all His kids too.

I saw a cartoon once that pretty well described us. One guy was holding a shotgun. The guy on the other side of the fence was saying, *"Don't shoot! We may both be on the same side."*

# 5

## GRACE IS AROUND HERE SOMEWHERE!

I will never forget the day I was baptized into Christ. Jan. 16, 1944. South San Antonio church of Christ. "South San" as it was affectionately called. Twelve years old. Sincere, but scared to death! I was as genuine as you can be about taking Jesus as my Lord. My daddy baptized me with his own hands. Strong hands. Hands rough from work on the railroad where he built box cars. I can still see his lips trembling as he asked me, "Son, do you believe Jesus Christ is the Son of God?" "I do!" Dad raised his hand and repeated these words heard at nearly every baptism. "By the authority of our Lord and Savior Jesus Christ, and in obedience to His command, I now baptize you in the name of the Father, and of the Son and of the Holy Ghost." I was under, back up, and brand new!

That's still the way it's done! That's biblical and like all the conversions of the book of Acts. Customs and cultures change. But that's the marvelously simple and simply marvelous way people become children of God.

Back in those days we were all pretty legalistic. There was a strong demand for "book, chapter and verse" for all we believed and practiced. And, may I add, that's still the way it should be. But it was deeper than that. There was heavy emphasis on works, duty and doctrine. We didn't hear much about faith, grace, joy and love.

It was an era of arguing with our religious neighbors and debating with any and every denominational preacher we could talk into it. I must have attended a dozen debates by the time I was baptized into Christ. Furthermore, I remember trouble within the church over doctrinal matters.

I've mentioned earlier my family's attendance at a little "one cup" church in Verdi, Texas. My dad was not of that persuasion but we had an uncle there. They had no preacher and my dad loved to preach. So for a time dad worked at his job on the Missouri Pacific Railroad and we drove to Verdi on weekends. These trips were mostly pleasurable. We got out into the country, visited with cousins, hunted in their pastures and attended the little one cup church.

Well, it wasn't long before it became clear that some of the "communion set" brethren didn't take to dad preaching for the "one-cuppers." Dad was blasted from the pulpit (by *name*) for fellowshipping the "anti's." It broke dad's heart and we tearfully left our home church in "South San"! When dad wasn't preaching in Verdi we would drive across town to another congregation where dad wouldn't be criticized. I did not at the time realize it might have been an omen for my own later criticism for "fellowshipping the instrumentals."

Two things dominated our church lives in those days prior to my own preaching ministry. One, we were taught to argue. And argue we did. My early childhood is filled with memories of arguments at the church building, in our own home and other people's homes that lasted into the night.

The other thing that dominated my early religious experience was the fact that we couldn't disagree without dividing. "If I am right then you're wrong, lost and headed for Hell!" And in those days I didn't know anything about essentials and non-essentials. This was the way we reasoned whether the issue was baptism or serving in the army. We argued cups, classes, located preachers, colleges, orphan homes, centralized control, institutionalism, choirs, instrumental music, pastors, *ad infinitum.*

My early view of the church was so narrow. I often imagined that there couldn't be more than a dozen or so "faithful gospel preachers" and surely no more than a thousand or so saved people in the world. Didn't the Bible say, "And if the righteous scarcely be saved . . ." (I Pet. 4:18, KJV)?

## THE BEGINNING OF MY MINISTRY!

I began to preach in September of 1949 the week before I turned 18. I had been in our preacher boys' class every Monday night for several moths. One of the boys got me an assignment for the next Sunday in Cotulla, Texas. I made that 170 mile round trip every week for the next two years. Working in the bank where I was a teller during the week; preaching on Sunday. I did "fill-in" preaching in a number of places for the next few years. During this time I went into the United States Air Force and was sent to Korea. About a dozen servicemen worshipped in the little chapel on the flight line and I preached for them. After my discharge from the service in 1955 I began my first full time ministry in Stockdale, Texas. Next preaching assignments were in Siloam Springs, Ark., and then I did a missionary stint in Perth, Western Australia.

## AUSTRALIA AND GRACE!

It was in Australia I was to meet up with a Biblical emphasis I had somehow missed in my previous years as a Christian. I was visiting with a lovely elderly couple one afternoon. Wes said to me, "Ah Marvin, isn't Isa. 40:31 a beautiful verse?" I said, "What does it say?" "You don't know?" He seemed shocked. Well, I don't think you have to memorize Isa. 40:31 to go to heaven. But it is a marvelous verse. It says,

> But those who hope in the Lord will renew their strength. They will soar on wings like eagles. They will run and not grow weary, they will walk and not be faint!

I not only didn't know what Isa. 40:31 says. I didn't know any verses on love, grace, joy or excitement.

## MY UNDERLINED BIBLE!

Back in preacher boys' class we learned to underline our Bibles. I had dozens of verses underlined and committed to memory. Can you guess what they were? They were all the verses to win arguments with my denominational friends. Now lest someone should accuse me of no longer believing these verses let me clarify. Those verses still teach exactly what they taught so long ago. My convictions didn't change But my *emphasis* did! You see, Hell is a fact but heaven is the emphasis. Jesus did not come to condemn the world but to save it (cf. John 3:17).

Since that day I've discovered many marvelous verses on the love, grace and mercy of God. I have learned that love, joy and grace are the emphasis of the Bible. I still believe and preach every line in the Word of God. But my emphasis has changed. And most assuredly I've gone out of the judging business. I will preach the Word of God without compromise. But I'll try to make my emphasis the same as His and I'll try to leave all the judging to the only One qualified.

## A CHANGED MAN; A HAPPY MAN!

I am sure my experiences in Australia changed me. I am equally sure my continued study of the Bible gave me a different perspective than I had in the early days of my Christianity. For one thing I'm not afraid of the verses on grace anymore. I feel no need to qualify or add a disclaimer when I'm quoting "for it is by grace you have been saved" (Eph. 2:8). I now realize that all the works I may do will never make me deserve the salvation that God gave me *"anyway"*! All my "rightness" in doctrine, the money I give, or the souls I lead to Christ will not make me deserve what my Jesus did for me. Heaven is what I get; not what I deserve! It is indeed "Amazing Grace" that saved a wretch like me!

## MY LIFE SINCE GRACE TOOK OVER!

The more I understood grace, the more several things changed in my life and ministry. To my surprise I found myself preaching about the same things I always did. I believe the Bible is the inspired Word of God. I preach Jesus as Lord. I rejoice in the church as God's agency of reconciliation. I believe all the saved are added to the church upon the new birth. But now I see that grace is the greatest motivator of works and service! Far from being "easy salvation," grace draws, insists and demands. How can anyone recognize what God has done for him without giving his all to the Lord? As in the song, "When I Survey the Wondrous Cross," it demands "my soul, my life, my all!"

I find an ease with people with whom I disagree. Especially preachers. Nor is this compromise. Grace, like love, casts out fear (I John 4:18). And it opens doors of opportunity I never had when I was a legalist. I won't call others "legalists" but I will call myself one. I was saved but I was a

47

legalist. Once I was inhibited; now I'm *inhabited*!

I was asked to speak on a panel composed of a Catholic priest, a Unitarian minister, a Jewish rabbi and myself. The subject was "What I believe and Why!" After our brief speeches the audience reacted to us with questions and comments. It was lively to be sure. Years ago I could never have done it. Today I thrive on it. I've lost my fear. Truth has nothing of which to be afraid! And the more sure you are of what you believe, the less fearful of anyone's attack. It is a marvelous feeling!

Another thing has changed in my ministry. I will preach anywhere I'm asked. My more conservative brothers take me to task for "preaching among the instrumentals" etc. I believe it is fair to ask that people judge me by *what* I say not *where* I say it!

I participate vigorously in the annual Restoration Forums. These talks between brethren in the Independent Christian churches and churches of Christ are a marvelous experience. We explore areas we have in common. And it is refreshing to find that we have much more in common than areas where we disagree. It is exciting to find others as interested in being Biblical, following Jesus, and building churches that please our Lord!

Those who have been scripturally baptized have been born into the same family. Vertical unity brings horizontal unity! If God has added us as saved people to His family the very least we can do is try to love and understand one another. I will commit my life to a pursuit of preserving the fellowship of the Family of God and a commitment to following His precious Word the Bible!

Well, there's my story. One man's trip from drudgery to delight. One pilgrim's journey from *enduring* to *enjoying* his Christianity. Nor is the journey over. For success is a journey not a destination. If these pages make you think, I am grateful. If they make you re-examine, I am glad! Instead of croaking like crows we should be singing like nightingales! And flying like eagles!

# 6

## HUMAN-EUTICS, I

Many of our differences, especially among those who accept the Bible as the inspired, infallible Word of God, come from the fact that our standard of understanding Bible authority is different.

Thus "Hermeneutics," or as I have styled this chapter, *"human-neutics"*! And you will shortly see why! The text book on this subject was written by Prof. D.R. Dungan many years ago. I have been unable to find a date of its first publication. But all segments of the Restoration Movement have read and studied it carefully. Oddly enough it was published by The Standard Publishing Company of Cincinnati, Ohio. This is the publishing center of the Independent Christian churches. My copy of the book has a sticker showing I bought mine from W.W. Stirman Bibles and Books of Waco, Texas. Stirman was a noted leader in the non-instrumental churches of Christ. That in itself is very interesting.

Hermeneutics is defined as the "science of interpretation"! It is our system of understanding what the Bible teaches. Which examples in the Bible are binding? What things are authorized? Which things are excluded? In short hermeneutics is our way of deciding what we believe and practice from the Bible. We will come up with a standard by which we can form a conclusion or else we will have to have someone write out for us exactly what we are to believe and practice. We will now discuss the hermeneutical approach to the Bible as practiced by the three major segments of the Restoration Movement.

## THE DISCIPLES OF CHRIST!

This hermeneutic is held by the Disciples of Christ churches. They are identified usually by a sign which reads *"First Christian Church; Disciples of Christ."* They do not accept a literal interpretation of scripture. It is commonly believed that the Bible contains myths and allegories never to be taken literally. It is common among Disciples preachers to reject the virgin birth of Jesus, authority and inspiration of scripture and the necessity of baptism by immersion. They practice "open membership" which means they will accept anyone's baptism if that person is happy with it! I will not go into any more lengthy detail of this hermeneutic as both Independent Christian churches and churches of Christ vehemently reject this as a valid way of interpreting scripture.

## NON-INSTRUMENTAL CHURCHES OF CHRIST!

Both the non-instrumental churches of Christ and the Independent Christian churches take a far more fundamental approach to Biblical interpretation. In fact in a recently published survey it was shown that these two groups have an 85% agreement on a sampling of 100 issues. Both would share only about a 15% agreement with the Disciples churches.

Both these fellowships lay heavy stress to the following verses:

"the very word which I speak will judge" (John 12:48)
"the scriptures are 'God-breathed' " (II Tim. 3:16,17)
"men spoke from God as they were carried along by the Holy Spirit" (II Pet. 1:20,21)
"the dead (will) be judged by (what was) recorded in the books" (Rev. 20:12,13).

Just here it might be good to explore how we come up with a hermeneutic in the first place. It naturally comes in the search for answers to some honest and necessary questions. How can we tell when a command is binding on us today? By what standard are we to know which things are included or excluded from our worship and service to God? Honest, God-fearing scholars wrestle for a solid way of knowing.

It is very important, at this point, to note that the hermeneutic arrived at is the process of a search by human beings. That's why these two chapters are called *"Human-eutics"*! Our hermeneutic is the product of honest, God-seeking scholars. It is *not* scripture. And it is *not infallible*! A belief that our hermeneutic is as valid as scripture itself is one of the most serious mistakes Christians have ever made. It is inductive in nature and comes from study, prayer, beliefs and scholarship of human beings. Their intentions were all good. But the fact that they are humans makes it a serious mistake to draw lines of fellowship based, not upon the scriptures themselves, but on the scholarship of these men.

## HOW "COMMAND, EXAMPLE, INFERENCE" EVOLVED!

Churches of Christ are widely known for their hermeneutic

which demands "direct command, approved example or necessary inference" for a doctrine or practice to be authorized in scripture!

Most fundamental Bible believers will conclude that what the Bible has commanded is just that — *commanded*! Commands are not optional! Thus when Jesus commanded in the great commission, "baptizing them" we come to the conclusion baptism is not optional. Further, Peter "commanded them to be baptized" (Acts 10:48). It is through this process that the famous "steps to salvation" are taught and practiced. Jesus Himself has commanded faith, repentance, confession and baptism (cf. John 8:24, Luke 13:3, Matt. 10:32, Mark 16:16). We would no more compromise these teachings than we would compromise the virgin birth of our Lord!

It is so important to recognize that the Independent Christian churches are with us 100% on this point in our hermeneutic. This is most significant when discussing our differences with them.

Now comes the matter of "approved example"! Exactly what is meant by this term? This hermeneutic implies that what was practiced with the approval of God by the early church gives us the authority to do the same. Some noted examples would be:

(1) Assembling on the first day of the week (Acts 20:7),
(2) Corporate worship with
   (a) handling of spiritual gifts!
   (b) women's role in the assembly (vs. 34),
(3) Giving (I Cor. 16:1,2),
(4) Communion (I Cor. 11:23-34).

"Approved example" is not without problems. How do you know the example is approved? We have the example of a young man, Eutychus, falling asleep in church (Acts 20:9). Some still follow that example although I'm sure no one believes this carries the approval of God. Which examples are binding?

54

Which are not? Which are cultural, which are incidental?

Communion (the Lord's supper) is a prime example. Every time we read of observing communion, including the night Jesus instigated it, the disciples were in an "upper room." Are we to conclude communion can only be taken upstairs? The only instruction I know about when to partake of the communion is in the following passage:

> "When you come together to eat, wait for each other" (I Cor. 11:33).

Are we to conclude the Lord's supper is a matter for Sunday only? *One time alone?* Excluding taking communion to the sick and shut in? Excluding a second offering of the communion on Sunday night for those who were not in the morning assembly? You see it is easy to prove too much by "approved example"!

We move next to "necessary inference"! Let's take a common command of the Old Testament to illustrate our point. The Jews were commanded to "Remember the Sabbath day by keeping it holy" (Exod. 20:8)! Nowhere did the Bible say remember *every* Sabbath day. But the Jews knew every week had a Sabbath day. And every Sabbath that rolled around they were faced with the command to "keep it holy"! We have also used this line of reasoning on "weekly" observance of the Lord's supper and the necessity of a church treasury!

This hermeneutic is the key reason churches of Christ do not use instrumental music in Christian worship. There is no command. There is no example (approved or otherwise) for its use. And its practice is nowhere "inferred" in scripture!


## COMMENTS ON THE NON-INSTRUMENTAL HERMENEUTIC!

Just what about this hermeneutic commonly practiced by churches of Christ? Pretty good if I do say so myself! By that hermeneutical process we've been able to make a strong stand as a people who love God and have high regard for Bible authority. From this doctrinal stance we've been able to serve hurting people and save lost people from their sins!

But is it *the* hermeneutic? Is it fool proof and 100% accurate? May we, must we, divide from and refuse fellowship with all who don't adhere to this standard? Must we "mark and avoid" those who love God and believe in the authority of His word as much as we do? Just because they don't follow our hermeneutic to the letter?

I appeal for a new look! Not a new hermeneutic! A brother wrote a little tract called "The Current Unity Movement." He doesn't like the Restoration Forums where brethren who disagree get together for study and prayer. He thinks we have decided on a "new hermeneutic." It is *his* term. To my knowledge the term "new hermeneutic" has never been used at any of the Restoration Forums. I have never heard anyone call for a new hermeneutic. But I have heard a plea for more study, more prayer and a better attitude toward those who sincerely differ from us. I have never heard a cry for compromise of personal convictions.

As Milton Jones (Seattle, Wa.) has said, "You will have a hermeneutic or you'll have a creed!" But let's please understand God did not say "you must have a command, example or inference"! Our hermeneutic is no more infallible than theirs. Truth has nothing of which to be afraid. Let us boldly restudy our hermeneutic. Are there any flaws? Any loop holes? Let's continue (chapter seven) by examining the hermeneutic of our instrumental brethren. It just might be revealing!

# 7

## HUMAN-EUTICS, II

You must read the previous chapter for this chapter to make any sense. In chapter six we began a discussion of hermeneutics (the science of interpretation). Two things are very important:
1. You have to have a hermeneutic or someone will have to write you a creed! Otherwise you won't know what to believe!
2. A hermeneutic is not scripture; it is *not* infallible!
We then took a look, briefly, at the hermeneutic of the Disciples of Christ churches. Then a more lengthy look at that of the non-instrumental churches of Christ. We will now attempt at least as lengthy a discussion of the hermeneutic of the Independent Christian churches.

### INDEPENDENT CHRISTIAN CHURCHES!

Several things are important to know about the group

known as "Independent Christian Churches." You will make serious mistakes in identifying them if you do not know these things. First of all the signs in front of their church buildings often say, "First Christian Church." The untrained observer will not know that the Disciples of Christ churches also commonly use this designation. Thus they are regularly mistaken for a group that holds a much looser view of Bible authority, practices open membership, accepts sprinkling as baptism, has women preachers and many other things.

Independent Christian churches commonly believe in the same "essentials" believed and taught in churches of Christ, i.e.

1. The being and authority of God!
2. The Lordship of Jesus Christ!
3. The inspiration and authority of the Bible!
4. The grandeur and glory of the church!
5. Baptism as essential to the new birth!
6. Genuine commitment to the will, way and word of God!

They are equally zealous to practice a hermeneutic that leads to an exact and faithful following of the word of God! Their study, prayer and scholarship leads them to the following hermeneutic. It is three-point like that of the non-instrumental brethren! I will state it all together and then proceed to explain it!

1. Scriptural!
2. Unscriptural!
3. Anti-scriptural!

Scriptural, to them, is the same as when the non-instrumentals say "command." By scriptural they mean "what is instructed of God" or "commanded by Him." There is total agreement on both sides that when something is commanded of God it forever settles the matter. These things must be taught and practiced!

Unscriptural! This is where we have to pay close attention. The same thing is not meant by both groups using this term. To the non-instrumentals unscriptural means "unauthorized" therefore sinful! By the term "unscriptural" Christian churches merely mean "not mentioned in scripture." It is extremely important to know this. Therefore they will refer to the following things as "unscriptural": *song books, public address systems, church buildings, instrumental music, communion sets, contribution plates!*

Now watch what these brethren do when a thing is not Scriptural (commanded), and is Unscriptural (not mentioned). They see if it is *Anti-scriptural*, that is prohibited by scripture. Anything the scripture forbids is of course dropped immediately.

Thus, on the subject of using instrumental music in worship, they reason:

"Is it scriptural (commanded)? No!"
"Is it unscriptural (not mentioned)? Yes!"
"Is it anti-scriptural (forbidden)? No!"

With such items ("unscriptural"), they believe they have the liberty to proceed with prayer and caution! A careful understanding of these two hermeneutics will add greatly to better communication and discussion between these fellowships and a pursuit of what to do about differences! It is not a matter of "one cares about Bible authority and the other does not." These two hermeneutics represent the best each fellowship can come up with in an effort to please God and faithfully follow His Word!

### RESTORATION FORUM #1; JOPLIN, MISSIOURI

I shouldn't be surprised that there has been a lot of criticism of the Restoration Forums. This has come basically from the non-instrumental ranks. But I frankly find it hard to understand. We preach on unity more than any religious group on earth but practice it less. We talk *about* one another but we are so reluctant to talk *with* each other! But I thank God for good brethren such as Don DeWelt and Alan Cloyd who were so "instrumental" (no pun intended) in putting on Restoration Forum #1 in Joplin, Missouri, August 7-9, 1984.

Cloyd and DeWelt were part of a growing number of brethren on both sides who are dissatisfied that we are not talking with each other. We teach the same plan of salvation. That means Jesus has added us to the same church (His church, Acts 2:47). Now the fact that we're in the same church does not mean we are both right. In itself it doesn't mean we are both saved. But it does speak to us about the way we should treat one another. We talk about how we love the Father but we keep beating up on His kids. Cloyd and DeWelt thought it was about time those who wanted a loving exchange between "alienated" brethren should get the chance.

Compromise was never the aim! Merging the two fellowships together was not intended. It is not even possible! Fellowship is a personal thing. One brother to another. One disciple with the Father!

Fifty brethren from each fellowship were invited to the first forum. Effort was made to get a representation of the views of the mainstream. And then a format was decided upon that would give an honest and fair exchange of the convictions of both groups and a chance for loving discussion. There were no strings on what could be said. To the contrary, speakers were urged to plainly state their convictions and concerns, but also to attempt to "speak the truth in love" (Eph. 4:15). The Christian churches were represented by such notable brethren as Don DeWelt, Victor Knowles, Ken Idleman, Russell Boatman, and others. Church of Christ speakers included Reuel Lemmons, Monroe Hawley, Rubel Shelly, Hardeman Nichols, Buster Dobbs, Richard Rogers and others.

The format allowed for a maximum of discussion and information. A central area of concern would be addressed by a speaker from both fellowships. Then the group would break into groups of ten (five instrumental and five non-instrumental) for intense discussion of the two speeches. The fully assembled groups would then hear a report of these small group discussions. Another added blessing would be eating together, sharing the same motel, hearing singing groups (all without instruments), singing and praying together. The first of these was in Joplin, followed by Tulsa, Pepperdine, Milligan College, Cincinnati, Lincoln, and Akron. Restoration Forum VIII is planned for Nov. 7-9, 1990, at the Garnett church of Christ in Tulsa, Oklahoma, in case you read this book before that time! The public is enthusiastically invited to attend!


### WEAKNESS DISCOVERED IN BOTH HERMENEUTICS!

Back to the first forum in Joplin. It was in one of those small group discussions that I made two startling discoveries. At least they were startling for me. That's the beauty of personal, "one to one" discussions. What you believe gets tossed out there to see if it will stand the test of investigation. Truth, I say again, has absolutely nothing of which to be afraid.

We were looking at one another's hermeneutic. A non-instrumental brother said, "With your hermeneutic I'll bet you have a lot of problems with liberalism!" To our surprise our instrumental brother replied, "Yes, most of our problems seem to come from the direction of liberalism!" Then another brother said, "But with your (non-instrumental) hermeneutic, I'll bet you have a lot of problems with 'fractionism'!" Touche! We in churches of Christ have insisted everyone follow our "command, example, inference" hermeneutic. Practically all churches heavily subscribe to this hermeneutic. It is the very basis of our strength. It is also the chopping block on which we have divided from the "one cup brethren," "non-class brethren," "non-institutional brethren," "no located preacher brethren" and a host of others.

They all use the same hermeneutic! They demand command, example or inference. And everyone to the right of us cuts off his more "liberal" brother using the same hermeneutic. In our own church directory, "Where the Saints Meet" we list by actual code some sixteen different kinds of churches of Christ who basically will not fellowship with other churches because of perceived violations of the *same hermeneutic*!

Now what shall we say to these things? Shall we abandon our hermeneutic? Has it been found faulty? Are we in need of another? Shall the instrumental brethren, because of the liberalism problems among them, abandon the "scriptural, unscriptural, anti-scriptural" hermeneutic in favor of ours? Cannot everyone see that these hermeneutics are basically good; the product of the best scholars we have in the world today? Cannot we also see that each has a weakness? Ours toward division among our own ranks! Theirs toward problems of liberalism!

Is a better hermeneutic to be found? I don't think so! I think what we are finding out is that nothing is infallible but the Word of God. God must have wanted us to keep studying, keep learning, and keep changing! It is enlightening that we agree wholeheartedly on what the Bible commands or instructs. Maybe God is showing us that while our convictions are sacred to us, they must never be used to run roughshod over brethren who disagree. I propose three things:

1. Let's stay united on what is commanded in scripture.
2. Congregations and individuals are going to have to decide some things through careful study and prayer!
3. Recognize there is no system whereby all issues will be solved for everyone!

Our convictions must not be compromised, but our fellowship must extend beyond our frail understanding of the Bible. Lines of fellowship must never be drawn as long as God-loving, Bible-believing brethren are struggling to please the

Father. If it is our accuracy and not His grace that saves us, we are of all men most miserable!

Plead your cause. Keep an open mind. Don't violate your conscience. Get all the fellowship you can get! Allow room for the convictions of others. Don't bind your "conclusions" on others! Don't draw lines of fellowship on steps two and three of either hermeneutic.

## A FRESH LOOK AT ROMANS 16:17,18

> Now I beseech you, brethren, mark them which cause divisions and offences contrary to the doctrine which ye have learned; and avoid them. For they that are such serve not our Lord Jesus Christ, but their own belly! (KJV)

This verse has been terribly abused and misappropriated by those who want to divide from all who disagree with themselves. It has been made to say, "Mark those who disagree or differ from us!" We have further argued, "They brought in the unauthorized practice; they caused the division!" But I beg you to consider that is precisely what the one cup brethren say of those who use communion sets; what the non-class people say of those who have Bible school. Surely it must make us think. Not every difference necessitates a division! It is not *difference* but *divisiveness* that is here spoken against!

Non-instrumental people don't have to begin using the instrument. Instrumental people don't have to "give up the instrument." When the matter is hermeneutical rather than a clear command of God let us allow each other the liberty of our convictions while we continue to study, pray and fellowship with each other as fallible but faithful children of God!

# 8

## LET'S KEEP EACH OTHER WARM!

### The Cold Within!

Six humans trapped by happenstance,
  in black and bitter cold;
Each one possessed a stick of wood,
  or so the story's told.

Their dying fire, in need of logs,
  the first woman held hers back.
For on the faces around the fire,
  she noticed one was black.

The next man looking cross the way,
  saw one not of his church,
And couldn't bring himself to give
  the fire his stick of birch.

The third one sat in tattered clothes,
  he gave his coat a hitch.

Why should his log be put to use
to warm the idle rich?

The rich man just sat back and thought
of the wealth he had in store;
And how to keep what he had earned,
from the lazy, shiftless poor.

The black man's face bespoke revenge,
as the fire passed from his sight.
For all he saw in his stick of wood,
was a chance to spite the white.

And the last man of this forlorn group
did naught except for gain.
Giving only to those who gave,
was how he played the game.

The logs held tight in death's still hands,
was proof of human sin.
They didn't die from the cold without,
they died from the cold within.

Author unknown

It is cold as I write this chapter. We've had a snowfall in Tulsa of 8 to 11 inches. Drifts have piled up in driveways. Up against walls it is four to five feet high. Icicles hang like glass daggers from the eaves of houses.

Inside, folks are trying to keep warm. Fireplaces are going. Puffy smoke rises from chimneys in the neighborhood. The lovely aroma of hackberry, oak and pecan is in the air.

You can almost see the families inside. Huddling together in front of their fireplaces. Trying to keep near the fire. Trying to keep close together. The thermostat on the wall is turned up to 80 degrees. We just want to stay warm. We want to keep each other warm.

People die in the cold. I think of all the old people living in sub-standard housing in the Tulsa area. I am quietly

66

reminded that when my wife pays the gas bill she always includes a bit extra which is used to keep the heat on in homes where they can't afford it. People will get stranded in their cars in many places. Some lose their way while walking in the woods. The cold is our enemy. And we must seek protection against it. Freezing to death. How awful!

But nothing could be so tragic as to freeze to death by choice! From the inside out! As if we had nothing better to do. As if "I'll show them!" Having my way! Proving my point! That's all that matters. That's the story in "The Cold Within!" This poignant little poem reminds us of the many prejudices we have today. And how we suffer rather than swallow our pride and help each other keep warm.

## RACIAL PREJUDICES!

I grew up with racial prejudices I didn't even know I had. San Antonio, Texas. Water fountains, rest rooms, theater balconies, seats at the back of the bus. All for "blacks only!" They couldn't use the ones reserved for whites. And all this time if anyone had asked me if I was prejudiced against blacks I would have steadfastly denied it! A.C. Christman, a late, great black preacher in Tulsa, was a good friend of mine. He once told me he had driven all night many times because he couldn't find a motel that would rent him a room.

But praise God, we're coming out of much of this prejudice. Bus ministry has put us "out there where Jesus was." Kids of all races believe you're sincere when you come into their communities asking them to ride the Joy Bus on Sunday! Bus ministry did three things for the Garnett church where I preach. It got us out of apathy. It put us out there where Jesus did His ministry, and put us in the "people ministry." "All" people!

The Garnett church is an integrated church in every sense.

We have all races, all ages, all circumstances worshipping God together. And we have found this is the secret of really being a happy family. It is a cold world; and we're just trying to keep each other warm.

## OTHER KINDS OF PREJUDICE!

There is social prejudice. Their kind. Our kind. You see, prejudice is just "difference." We are suspicious and wary about anything different from the way we look and the way we do things!

There is educational prejudice. Those with it look down on those without it. The uneducated believe the educated are snobs. The educated believe they are superior to those who never went to school. Consequently we isolate from one another. We are suspicious of one another. The resultant cold nearly freezes us to death. We've got to find a way to keep each other warm!

There is religious prejudice. Perhaps this is the coldest of them all. We can and should hold our convictions as sacred. Still we could be nice to each other. We could fellowship each other and learn from each other. Within a local church we must learn to get along. We've got to trust each other. We need to give love, acceptance and forgiveness. It's cold out there in the world. God's people need to help each other keep warm.

## THE BIBLE AND PREJUDICE!

Prefacing the four marvelous stories of the lost sheep, lost coin and the two lost boys, Jesus set the example for "togetherness!"

Now the tax-collectors and sinners were all gathering around to hear him. But the Pharisees and the teachers of the law mut-tered. This man welcomes sinners and eats with them. (Luke 15:1,2)

A large audience had gathered to hear Jesus preach. But there was prejudice in the group. Some said, "How can he allow people like that to associate with people like us?" Jesus was quick to show them no one had the right to look down their noses at other people. They were all sinners. They all needed a savior. And praise God, they had a God Who was willing to save anyone!

From Matthew 22:9,10 we are instructed:

Go to the street corners and invite to the banquet anyone you find. So the servants went out into the streets and gathered all the people they could find, both good and bad, and the wed-ding hall was filled with guests.

Notice Jesus wants everyone at His banquet. How dare a church be more exclusive than Jesus Christ? If His grace in-cludes me how dare any man exclude me. They lived in a cold, cold world. So do we! And we see Jesus inviting them in to get warm. Yea, to keep each other warm.

There's another passage we should look at:

My brothers, as believers in our glorious Lord Jesus Christ, don't show favoritism. Suppose a man comes into your meeting wearing a gold ring and fine clothes, and a poor man in shabby clothes also comes in. If you show special attention to the man wearing fine clothes and say, 'Here's a good seat for you,' but say to the poor man, 'You stand there,' or 'Sit on the floor by my feet,' have you not discriminated among yourselves and become judges with evil thoughts? (James 2:1-4)

What color is God? Since He is not partial to any color or race, neither should we be! Heaven is a mixed neighborhood. We must learn that the church is a place where we help keep each other warm! The sooner we learn this the greater will be the blessing of God on our efforts.

## OTHER LESSONS FROM THE POEM!

We need each other. As surely as those six people huddled around the fire needed each other, so do we. We must choose to trust one another, to give each other benefit of doubt.

Cooperation is essential to our mutual good. We selfishly hold on to what is "ours," and we die in the process. I cannot make it without you. You can't make it without me. Our stubbornness, our failure to admit this, has kept us in the cold. Differences are to be met with understanding, love and acceptance rather than suspicion, hatred and violence. It is time to swallow our pride, admit our need, and surround each other with our warmth!

Unity is great and needed. Sameness is unnecessary. My way is not the only way. My kind is not the only kind. Working together is the only way to success. If we all work together we can work it out. This certainly applies in the matter of religious conflict. Especially among those who share belief in the same "essentials!"

There's too much cold out there! Too much misunderstanding, too much separation, divorcing, dividing. *Don't shoot! We may both be on the same side!* We all have *one* God! He only has *one* Son! He brought *one* gospel; bought only *one* church! He issued *one* invitation. "Come to me *all* you who are weary and burdened and I will give you rest" (Matt. 11:28). It's time we dropped our suspicions of one another, our isolation from each other, our coldness toward one another.

Let's get together!

Let's stop the fighting!

Let's start uniting!

We may freeze from the cold without. But let's not die from the cold within!

# 9

## LEARNING TO DISAGREE WITHOUT DIVIDING!

They had such a sharp disagreement that they parted company. (Acts 15:39)

Scripture says they had a "sharp disagreement." Paul and Barnabas. These two grand old giants of the faith. And it threatened their future work for God. Unless resolved they could no longer work together.

The problem? His name was John Mark, nephew to Barnabas. Uncle Barny wanted to take nephew Johnny on the first missionary journey with him and Paul. But he was a quitter. We're not treated to the reason he quit. But it was sufficient to convince Paul that he should not be taken again. So when Barnabas proposed a second trip and wanted to take Johnny, Paul objected. They "sharply" disagreed! So Paul chose Silas and headed north. Barnabas took John Mark and headed west. And the Bible says these two teams were "commended by the brothers to the grace of God" (Acts 15:40). The cause between them was greater than the disagreement between them. And later when Barnabas' judgment was proven right, Paul sent for John Mark saying "he is helpful to me in my ministry" (II Tim. 4:11).

## TROUBLE IN THE CHURCH!

The early church had its problems. The first was functional; the second was doctrinal. In Acts 6 there was a complaint that certain widows were overlooked in their benevolent program. The second was more serious. Certain teachers came to Antioch teaching that unless all male members were circumcised "you cannot be saved" (Acts 15:1). Here is as serious a problem as the church has ever faced. Scripture was being violated. Demands were being made by some members of the church to be imposed on other. "And you can't be saved if you don't!" Wow!

There followed the conference in Jerusalem to discuss this matter. Paul and Barnabas were there. The apostles and elders attended. In fact they got the whole church involved in the meeting (v. 22). And the matter was resolved by restating the essentials. By declaring no one had the right to impose circumcision (or any other law) on others! The point is, the matter was resolved without everyone being convinced. You know this because later on some Jewish Christians were still trying to impose circumcision on other Christians (cf. Gal. 2:3-5). It is also worthy to note that this matter was resolved without a church split.

In fact, two of the greatest cultural differences that ever existed were in the first century church. That of Jew and Gentile; that of slave and master. And scripture is full of the resultant problems of these Christians and their struggles together. Yet without a single mention of a church split, or of one congregation branding another! Such ungodly things simply were not done. The Bible closes at the end of the first century without anything closely kin to our practice today of "three main branches of the Restoration Movement," or "sixteen different kinds of churches of Christ!" It's time we took another hard look at the Word of God.

## THINGS TO PREACH IF OUR LIVES DEPENDED ON IT!

To be sure there are some things that must be preached and never compromised. Scripture says Jesus is God's "one and only Son" (John 3:16). There can be no argument about God having "another son," or a daughter! This simply cannot be disputed. It's like that bumper sticker I saw once that said, *"God said it, I believe it, that settles it!"*

Again, the Bible says, "man is destined to die once and after that to face judgment" (Heb. 9:27). The re-incarnationists can write all the books they want, man dies but once. We will surely face God in judgment no matter how many people may claim there is no life after death.

I took about a year going back through the Bible to hunt "the essentials." What things really matter? What things are matters of opinion? I came up with a list of six essentials. They will be discussed more than once in this book. That is both a matter of intention and importance. Rubel Shelly makes his "essentials list" the seven ones of Ephesians 4:4-6 (one body, Spirit, hope, Lord, faith, baptism and God). With that I have no quarrel. It is simply another way of stating essential things.

My list is as follows:
1. The Being of God, Hebrews 11:6
2. The Lordship of Jesus, John 8:24
3. The Inspiration and Authority of Scripture, II Timothy 3:16,17

4. The Grandeur and Glory of the Church, Ephesians 5:23-25
5. The New Birth, John 3:5; Romans 6:3,4
6. Genuine commitment to God's Will and Word! Revelation 2:10

For all the beauty and importance of unity, these things must be preached at all cost. The scripture reference beside each declares you cannot be saved unless you believe and follow. Division is a must with any who will not accept any one of the six!

*A WEAKNESS AMONG RESTORATION CHURCHES!*

These essentials are the strength of the people of God. We have debated our cause with the opposition. These are the "clear call of the trumpet" (I Cor. 14:8); the call to attack for the army of God.

But unfortunately many people in restoration churches never learned to disagree over *anything* without dividing! They put all teaching on the same level. It is almost like teaching if marriage is right then we all have to be married. No room was left for matters of opinion. Romans 14 and 15 were as if they were not part of the Bible. We said, "If two brothers disagree on *any* issue, at least one must be wrong, in violation of scripture and lost! We argued with him and withdrew fellowship from him.

My good friend John Whitehead has written a poignant little tract on this. He writes down about 200 issues over which contemporary Christians argue. He asks the reader to check in one of three columns about each issue:

1. This is a matter of faith and must be believed and practiced!
2. This is a matter of opinion over which we may disagree!

3. I cannot tell!

He then challenges the reader to try to find one other Christian in the world who fills out the tract exactly as he or she did! That is so eye-opening. It must dawn on us that there aren't any two Christians in the world who see every issue eye to eye! Are we to conclude there is only one "right, saved" person on earth?

## WE ALREADY FELLOWSHIP THOSE WITH WHOM WE DISAGREE!

Those who insist that we see every issue exactly alike do not realize how inconsistent they are. Not to mention how unrealistic. Let me give you a few examples. There will be people in the same congregation who feel differently about Christians serving in the military. Some won't serve at all. Some go in but refuse combat service. They usually serve in the medical corps. Some elect to work in munitions plants and manufacture the bullets that other Christians shoot. These who differ strongly are usually able to fellowship and serve in the same congregation.

In some churches there are those who support orphan homes and such cooperative efforts as radio and television programs. There are others whose consciences won't allow this, believing that no two churches may cooperate in a joint effort. But so long as "church money" is not used, they usually find a way to remain together.

Now on the matter of instrumental music in worship, let me surprise you. You probably cannot find two members of any *non-instrumental* church who agree on every aspect of this subject. Answer the following eight questions according to your convictions. Then see how many others agree with your answers:

1. Do you object to having a piano in your home?

2. Would you play religious songs on your home piano?
3. Would you listen to instrumental gospel cassettes?
4. Would you visit a church service where instrumental music will be played?
5. Would you sing if you visited such a service?
6. Would you object to organ music at a wedding?
7. Would you object if it is not in a church of Christ building?
8. Would you "sing along" to instrumental religious songs on radio or television?

### POSSIBLE SOLUTIONS!

We can and should have "unity of the faith" but we can never have unity in all matters. So our job is to decide which things belong to "faith" and which to "liberty." Especially when two groups such as the churches of Christ and the Independent Christian churches have such a sacred regard for Bible authority I suggest five things:

1. If the matter is not essential to salvation, don't make it a matter of prime importance!
2. Never draw lines of fellowship with those whose aim is the same as ours: that of honoring the Lordship of Jesus, and the inspiration and authority of His Word. *Unless they violate one of the six essentials!*
3. Allow a brother or church freedom when his practice does not bind you to a personal violation of conscience. For example: military service, raising hands, clapping, saying, "Amen, Praise the Lord!" singing during communion, special contributions to things you don't agree with!
4. In matters that "include and involve" you in practices that violate your conscience, do not participate, but respect the brother's freedom! For example: whole

assembly instructed to stand, hug, raise hands, clap etc.

5. Do stay together, keep studying, keep talking, keep praying, keep fellowshipping and keep winning souls! In short, keep doing all we can do together without violation of conscience. We need all the fellowship we can get!

Ephesians 4:3 says, "Make every effort to keep the unity of the Spirit through the bond of peace." Unity of the Spirit comes a lot easier when there is a spirit of unity!

# 10

## "IN ESSENTIALS, UNITY: IN OPINION, LIBERTY; IN ALL THINGS LOVE!"

Preach the word; be prepared in season and out of season (II Tim. 4:2).

There is no more stirring verse in the Bible to restoration preachers. It's a battle cry. It's like, "Remember the Alamo!" The first nine verses of that chapter call us to duty. The Word must be preached. All the Word! Nothing but the Word! We are warned that men will tire of sound doctrine. They will want their ears tickled with more soothing and palatable ideas. And sadly, they will find teachers who will tell it the way they want it! But you, young Timothy, stick to the book! Paul was ready to live (or die) for Jesus!

### RESTORATION SLOGANS!

I'm walking on holy ground! In this chapter we're taking a

sober look at the slogans of restoration fathers to whom we owe so much. Great men! Mighty men who didn't call attention to themselves. They called men to follow God and His Word. Their aim was to bring to an end the shameful religious division of their day and unite God's people on the Bible.

Great slogans punctuated this exciting era in the latter half of the nineteenth century. Slogans like:

Let us speak where the Bible speaks,
And remain silent where it is silent.
Let us call Bible things by Bible names,
And do Bible things Bible ways!

Preaching of the Bible only makes Christians only!

In matters of faith, let us have unity;
In matters of opinion, let us have liberty;
And in all things, charity!

In more recent times other great slogans have been added:

God wanted what He wrote, and wrote what He wanted!

We need book, chapter and verse for what we believe and practice!

Let's take a closer look at the slogan under consideration at this time:

*In matters of faith let us have unity!*

This is the only area where we have the right to demand unity. By "matters of faith" we mean those things clearly commanded in scripture. They are not a matter of deduction. God has clearly and emphatically commanded them. They are not up for discussion. They are not optional. They must surely be believed or we are lost!

There are not as many of these as some have supposed.

Elsewhere we have mentioned the "six essentials." We now take a closer look.

## ONE: THE BEING OF GOD!

And without faith it is impossible to please God, because anyone who comes to him must believe that he exists and that he rewards those who earnestly seek him. (Heb. 11:6)

Accepting the authority and existence of God is not optional. Two qualifications are clearly listed in the above verse for salvation. We must (1) believe God exists, and (2) earnestly seek him!

## TWO: THE LORDSHIP OF JESUS!

Jesus answered, I am the way and the truth and the life. No one comes to the Father except through me!" (John 14:6)

There is no way to get to heaven except through Jesus. We heartily admire the many benevolent works of Jewish people. There are many good people in religions who do not accept the divinity and Lordship of Jesus. But while we admire them and do not wish to be harsh and narrowminded, there is only "one way" to the Father! And that way is Jesus! To reject this "faith" is to reject salvation!

## THREE: THE INSPIRATION AND AUTHORITY OF THE BIBLE!

And I saw the dead great and small, standing before the throne, and books were opened. Another book was opened, which is the book of life. The dead were judged according to what they had done as recorded in the books! (Rev. 20:12)

There are many other scriptures to put with this one to show that the Bible is the inspired, infallible Word of God (cf. II Tim. 3:16,17; John 12:48)! We will one day stand before God in judgment (Heb. 9:27). God has a giant balance scales. Our lives will be placed on one side; the Bible on the other! Where we are sentenced for eternity depends on what we have done with the Word of God! Serious stuff! Not an option as we travel from the cradle to the grave to eternity!

## FOUR: THE GLORY AND IMPORTANCE OF THE CHURCH!

For the husband is the head of the wife as Christ is the head of the church, his body, of which he is the Savior! (Eph. 5:23)

The church belongs to Jesus Christ! He paid for it with His blood! It is the body to which Jesus adds all saved people (Acts 2:47). The church is not the savior. But every saved person is in it! It is not optional. When Jesus comes for His own you need to be in the church of which He is the Savior!

## FIVE: THE NEW BIRTH!

Jesus answered, "I tell you the truth, unless a man is born of water and the Spirit, he cannot enter the kingdom of God!" (John 3:5)

Baptism is essential to salvation. Jesus has put it before remission of sins and salvation. It is *from* baptism that we rise to walk in new life (Rom. 6:4). The matter is not up for discussion. In every verse where baptism and any equivalent of salvation are mentioned, baptism is always first. This is a matter of faith! Let's have unity in it!

## SIX: GENUINE COMMITMENT TO CHRIST!

Now it is required that those who have been given a trust must
prove faithful! (I Cor. 4:2)

Followers of Jesus must be genuine. The one area where God
requires one hundred percent is in our intentions. We cannot
be perfect. But we can all be genuine in our efforts to follow
God's will, way and Word! We may err because we are
human. But faithfulness is not an option.

These are matters of faith. They do not give us as much
trouble as the next part of the slogan which we will now
discuss.

### "IN MATTERS OF OPINION, LET US HAVE LIBERTY!"

Our problems on this one are many! Just which things are
non-essential? Which are matters of opinion? Usually what I
think about a thing is faith. If you disagree, you have violated
the faith and are "wrong, unscriptural and lost"! How much
liberty am I to give?

This is why a good study of "Hermeneutics" is essential. I
have devoted two whole chapters in this book to "Human-
eutics"! The word "Hermeneutics" is taken from the Greek
"Hermes," the messenger of the gods; interpreter of Jupiter.
One who attempts to explain what God has said is a 'Herme-
neus," an interpreter. Unfortunately not all matters of the Bible are as clear as the six essentials I have listed above. When
God fearing men who love and reverence the Bible disagree,
some tolerance and patience must be practiced. It is the fer-
vent belief of this writer that all who cling to the six essentials
previously listed are saved! The umbrella of "genuine" and
"faithful" covers the mistakes that occur with our best efforts
because we are human and fallible. So I want to fervently urge

us not to draw lines of fellowship over matters of opinion.

### UNDERSTAND FELLOWSHIP!

Many have a problem associating with brothers with whom they disagree. They look upon this association as compromise of truth. They believe all such association is giving them "God speed" and therefore makes them "partakers of their evil deeds (II John v. 11). I believe that verse applies only to the "essential" things. Certainly not to every matter over which we disagree.

In the first place fellowship is not endorsement! Just think for a moment of the insanity of believing that if you associate with someone it means you sanction everything that person believes and practices. Just apply that to Jesus Who spent so much time with publicans and sinners. To be sure some of the Pharisees bought the "association/endorsement" philosophy. So they complained, "this man welcomes sinners and eats with them" (Luke 15:2).

There are really two levels of fellowship. There is first of all the "fellowship which you've been called into" (I Cor. 1:9). This happens when a person is baptized into Jesus Christ (Gal. 3:26,27). Every Christian is in "the fellowship"! Now this does not mean these are all right on every issue. Nor does it mean they are all saved. But they are all in the Family of God.

There is a second level of fellowship. *"Have no fellowship with the unfruitful works of darkness"* (Eph. 5:11, KJV). Please note this verse does not say "Have no fellowship with those with whom you disagree!" It says have no fellowship with "works of darkness"!

I'd like to explain this "limited fellowship" when we disagree on "issues"! William Kay Moser was a conscientious objector. He was sent to prison for refusing to serve in the military at the same time I went into the United States Air Force and was sent to Korea. We obviously disagree on the subject of military service. He wrote a book about his experience called "Be a Man, Son!" It is a splendid book with lots of good lessons in it. Now I can fellowship Moser as my brother even though I disagree with him on the question of military service. I would have no problem working with him in the church, having him preach in my pulpit. I would enjoy fellowshipping with the church where he preached. But if he wrote a tract on "Why Christians Should Not Serve in the Military!" I would refuse to help him distribute it. I would say "I can't fellowship you in that!"

In the same way we've got to learn to allow people the liberty of their convictions. Restoration churches have divided over many issues. That we would disagree was inevitable. But that we should have divided over these things was wrong and unnecessary. May we rethink the issue of "In matters of opinion, let's have liberty!"

## "IN ALL THINGS, LOVE!"

Most assuredly let us love in spite of differences! We seem to have trouble with this on all levels. We sometimes have trouble loving the lost. And sadly enough we also have trouble loving the saved. The Bible urges us to "speak the truth in love" (Eph. 4:15). Love is the proof we are the people of God. Let that love be expressed by holding firm our precious convictions. After all our convictions are the most sacred things we've got. But let's cling tenaciously to the essential things. Defer judgment to God on all non-essential matters. Let love define all you do in your service to Jesus Christ; and your treatment of those with whom you disagree.

# 11

## TODAY'S CHURCH AND THE BOOK OF ACTS!

We are forever faced with the need of comparing ourselves with the original. It is dangerous to cut successive rafters using the one before as a standard. By the time you've done this a dozen times or so the last board will be considerably longer than the first. Each board must be cut by the original. The standard!

One man claimed he had an axe dating back to the days of George Washington. The axe just didn't look that old. When pressed, he admitted his axe had had three new blades and five new handles. But besides this he said it was the same old axe. Much of what we do in religion is about that original.

The Family of God is much larger than most of us knows! God put the Ethiopian eunuch in the church before any Christian in his native land knew about it. And whether or not any church would accept his baptism. God's Family consists of all who have been scripturally born into it. None of God's children are perfect. Not all of them are even mature. Some may approach genius status! If so, I doubt if any of them know it. Others may be retarded. Not all of them are even saved. But the Father loves all His children. And all who love their Father must love one another. It is a command as essential as baptism!

## OUR ROOTS!

Alex Haley blessed the contemporary world with his book "Roots"! It was a marvelous effort to trace the heritage of black Americans. Its intention was to give them understanding, identity and pride.

The roots of the church of Christ today are in the second chapter of Acts. All that happened before Acts two pointed ahead to that chapter. All that has happened since points back to it. This chapter tells of the marvelous beginning of the church. It is more than the birthday of the church. It is the "standard" by which the church is always to be measured in every generation. If churches will faithfully lay themselves alongside this standard of measurement we will not get far astray. Not once, but regularly. If we are all using the same standard of measurement we will take on the same appearance. Following are some of the things leaping out at us from page one of the diary of the New Testament church.

## A WILLINGNESS TO RESPOND TO NEW TRUTH!

Judaism's roots were fifteen hundred years old. It was not easy for Jews to accept something new. Change never comes easy. They fought long and hard against accepting Jesus as Messiah. Why? Because He didn't measure up to the prophesies of the Old Testament? No! Because it represented newness and change. And when they couldn't shut Him out they nailed Him out!

But on Pentecost morning Peter sang a new song! Jesus was proclaimed as "raised from the dead"! His answer to the empty tomb was that God had raised this Jesus as both Lord and Christ. Peter's sermon was laced with Old Testament prophecy pinpointing Jesus as Messiah. The Holy Spirit baptized apostles spoke in fifteen languages they had never studied. It was too much. More specifically it was enough! "Brothers, what shall we do?" "Repent and be baptized!" And they did it too. Three thousand of them. On the same day! What a dynamic illustration of a willingness to respond to truth when it is presented.

It is so great to see lost people respond to Jesus when they learn about Him. It is equally great to see Christians willing to study, learn, grow and change as they more fully understand God's will for their lives.


## *"THEY DEVOTED THEMSELVES" (vs. 42)*

Devotion indicates a "giving over" in a particular direction. It includes emotions of joy and duty. And scripture says this devotion was to the "apostles' teaching, and to the fellowship, to the breaking of bread and to prayer." They were hungry for the things of God. There was an eagerness about their learning, doing and commitment. This is a far cry from "coming to church" and "doing as you please." How we need to restore devotion to the twentieth century church.


## *"FILLED WITH AWE!" (vs. 43)*

It's too bad about that word "awful"! Today it just means "terrible." Its original meaning was "full of awe"! Awe is that feeling you have when you see the Grand Canyon for the first time. Or look into the face of a new born child. It is a holy "wow"! Today's church has lost the awe!

We were on our way home from Australia in 1965. Our plane was flying north along the west coast of America. The pilot pointed out the lovely Mt. Rainier. We excitedly urged our three small children to look out the window to see this dazzling sight. They looked up from their comics. Took a bored look. And were back to Batman and Mickey Mouse.

The train was crawling across Australia. It is a boring trip. You can take a picture out the window every hour. It will be the same picture. Flat, treeless, colorless! The train swayed from side to side. You could hear the clackety-clack of the wheels. Everyone was bored stiff. Everyone except one man. He was wide-eyed with excitement. He kept saying "marvelous!" "Wonderful!" Finally one of his fellow passengers said to him, "Look mate, we're all bored stiff. You keep yelling and pointing. What is it with you?" The excited stranger explained. "I was blind until a few days ago. I had an operation and now I can see everything. What is boring to you is new and exciting to me!"

That's what we need in the church today. A fresh operation on our spiritual eyes. We've seen the marvelous things of God too often. Things that ought to be awe-inspiring to us aren't! We've stared at the light until we've become spiritually blind. "Lord open our eyes that we may see wonderful things in your law" (Psa. 119:18).


### "ALL THE BELIEVERS WERE TOGETHER" (vs. 44)

What a marvelous verse! What a beautiful word, together! God's people were Jew and Gentile. Male and female. Slave and owner! Yet they were all "one in Christ" (Gal. 3:26-28). They had all the differences we have today. They could have been branded liberal and conservative. Subsequent epistles in the New Testament tell us of their struggles to all "speak the same thing." They had all the human problems in the church we have today. Yet scripture says "All the believers were of one heart and mind" (Acts 4:32). Oh that today's church would learn how to "contend for the faith" without our bent for division in our own ranks.

## *"THEY HAD EVERYTHING IN COMMON" (vs. 44,45)*

The benevolent philosophy of early Christians was remarkable. Some people's idea is "what's yours is mine if I can get it!" Others practice, "what is mine is mine; stay away from it!" But the early church said "what's mine is yours if you need it!" Even to the selling of possessions and goods. "There were no needy persons among them" (Acts 4:34). This speaks of a cohesiveness, a closeness that the church of today would do well to emulate. Division among us would be rare indeed if this feeling existed among us!

## *"GLAD AND SINCERE HEARTS"! (vs. 46)*

Early Christians were a happy lot. Their positive attitude won the favor of their neighbors (vs. 47). They even rejoiced that they were able to suffer for Jesus (Acts 5:41). Joy was considered a "fruit of the spirit" (Gal. 5:22). A natural result of belonging to Jesus. The world doesn't care two figs about doctrine. They want to see the effect of the product on the consumer! What the world wants to see is the real thing. Christians today should have that same positive radiance. It should show up at home! It ought to shine in the work place. And it most assuredly ought to show up in worship assemblies. Church services ought to be celebrations of joy! Have

93

you noticed that not many people attend funeral services?

## "PRAISING GOD!" (vs. 47)

I still have to laugh at that old illustration. A man was visiting in a large fashionable church. He liked something the preacher said. He said, "Praise the Lord!" An usher tiptoed over and rebuked the man for his outburst. "I was just praising the Lord," he said. The usher retorted, "This isn't any place to praise the Lord!" But it is! Sometimes churches do their best to keep their people dignified. In fact some are downright petrified. Let's get praise back in our lives and in our worship assemblies. Take huge sections of time just to praise God for His magnificent goodness, love and mercy toward us! They did! Have you measured your worship by the Acts two standard lately?

## "EVERY DAY CONVERSIONS" (vs. 47)

*And the Lord added to their number daily those who were being saved!*

Jesus came to earth for one reason. To seek and save the lost (Luke 19:10). And this is the single mission of the church. The church will be found helping the poor. That is our nature. Christians will meet together for meals, fun and games. That is our social personality. But the singular purpose for the church is the saving of souls. They got serious about their task. That's why this verse says "daily additions." Nor was this an isolated example. In Acts 16:5 we read, "So the churches were strengthened in the faith and grew daily in numbers!" For us to be a New Testament church we must be aggressive in evangelism. People whose number one goal is to

94

win souls find it much easier to get along with others who share the same passion. This should speak volumes to us!

## DEVOTED TO PRAYER! (vs. 42)

The Jerusalem church was a praying church. They honored the Jewish custom of a daily prayer time at three in the afternoon (Acts 3:1). The most dynamic prayer session you'll ever read about was in Acts chapter four. They prayed for boldness. The place was shaken. They were filled with the Holy Spirit. And got what they asked for (vs. 31). Whew! They prayed when they ordained deacons (Acts 6:6). Stephen prayed as he died for preaching Christ (Acts 7:59). They prayed for Peter who was in prison. God heard and got him out (Acts 12:5). Prayer is the power and life blood of the church today.

## THEY BELIEVED IN CHRIST'S SECOND COMING!

The scene just before Pentecost was the ascension of Jesus (Acts 1:9-11). Christ's mission on earth was complete! He had been crucified and resurrected. He gave His marching orders to the church (Mark 16:15,16). He gathered His apostles on the Mount of Olives. They watched as a cloud received Jesus back to heaven. Angels promised, "This same Jesus, who has been taken from you into heaven, will come back in the same way you have seen him go into heaven"! This vision never left the church. And it never should.

Dear friends Jesus is coming soon! Let us live in view of this fact. Let us get serious about being the people we ought to be. Let's build the churches Jesus wants built. Let's do the work He wants us to do. Let's treat one another like brothers and sisters in the greatest Family on earth. Jesus will fix it all when He comes again. Let's live in joyful anticipation of Christ's second coming.

Maranatha!

# 12

## THE CHALLENGE FACING THE TWENTY-FIRST CENTURY CHURCH!

Yet I hold this against you: you have forsaken your first love.
Remember the height from which you have fallen! Repent and
do the things you did at first. (Rev. 2:4,5)

Remember Ephesus? Paul and the third missionary
journey. Acts chapter nineteen! Colorful and exciting beginning. Twelve re-baptisms. Holy Spirit power. Dynamic victory over idolatry in the capital city of the great goddess
"Artemis." Christianity made an impact. The people accepted
Jesus as Lord. They brought their books of black magic and
burned them in the public square. Value? One hundred thirty-
seven years' wages!

Remember Ephesus? Great elders! Paul's farewell sermon
in Acts Twenty was preached to them. And they loved Paul.
They wept with him; embraced him and kissed him "grieving
most that they would never see his face again" (Acts
20:37,38).

Remember Ephesus? And the book of Ephesians? Perhaps the greatest study in the entire Bible on the New Testament Church. Ephesians proclaims the church as the body of Christ (1:21,22), the agency of reconciliation (2:16), God's Family (3:15), one body (4:4), the bride of Christ (5:25) and the army of the Lord (6:10ff).

Remember Ephesus? Our last picture of this church is in Rev. 2:1-7. John says they had "left their first love"! Such a great beginning. Such a sad ending!

## GLIMPSE OF THE NEXT ONE HUNDRED YEARS!

Today's church is minutes from the twenty-first century. These are bold, challenging times. Ours is a hi-tech world. There is a "get-with-it" attitude in big business and government. Opportunity has never been greater. The church must meet the challenge. This is a time for force not fading. Courage not cowardice. Holding to the old paths in doctrine. Keeping up with the times in attitude and method.

These are times of religious change. Many more churches are now teaching baptism for the remission of sins. Two Baptist churches in Tulsa have ordained elders. I asked a preacher friend, "Why is your church called 'Victory Christian Center'? Is this an attempt to cover up your denominational identity?" He replied, "No. Our denominational name limits the people of God. We're trying to get away from all things that divide God's people. We just want to be the people of God. We don't want to be denominational!" Interesting isn't it!? There's even a national television program called "Restoration." And for all the things you may not agree with, it is refreshing to hear people urging us to be "Christians only." It sure reminds us of the words of Thomas and Alexander Campbell, Barton W. Stone and others of a century ago. The Restoration Movement isn't over. It has hardly begun.

Change is in the air. The fields are white unto harvest! But not for a fading, locked-in, legalistic church. The Restoration Plea is the greatest plea in the religious world. Let's match it with an attitude that is equally radiant, exciting and positive!

## WE'VE DONE A LOT OF THINGS RIGHT!

I do not want to be identified with those who feel the church has lost its way. Nor do I want to close my eyes to our need to change. John acknowledged the Ephesian church's hard work and perseverance. They had endured hardship for the name of Jesus and not grown weary (Rev. 2:2-4).

And Restoration churches have done a lot of things right too. We've preached a strong loyalty to God and Bible authority. I doubt that a religious group anywhere has a better trained pulpit ministry in the Word of God. Our preachers have been known for years for "quoting lots of scripture" when they preach. Their sermons have been heavily laced with Bible texts. They have preached the need to give "book, chapter and verse" for all we believe and practice. Despite any tendency to be legalistic our preachers basically know and preach The Book!

Our churches have a commendable desire to be right and do right! At workshops, college lectureships and retreats there is that strong desire to "examine yourselves to see whether you are in the faith" (II Cor. 13:5). And we've been highly involved in ministry. We've practiced small group ministries, support groups for hurting people and we are unusually receptive to the calls of the hurting around the world. Whether hunger in Ethiopia, hurricane in the east or earthquake in the west, churches of Christ usually have their presence felt, standing shoulder to shoulder with others of like mind.

The Tulsa International Soul Winning Workshop is our

brotherhood's largest gathering. Twelve thousand brethren from all over the world are encouraged to love, good works and evangelism.

### *"YET I HOLD THIS AGAINST YOU!" (vs. 4)*

We are not ready for the challenges of the twenty-first century without a serious look at our failings. We simply do not make an impact in our communities. Americans for the most part have never heard of us. Far too many of our churches are in decline. We have settled for the status quo. And while preaching to the world about religious unity, there is scarcely a church in America divided more than we! Worse yet, we seem to accept it! Efforts and interest of preachers and churches to "do something" about our differences have been met with criticism and outright opposition. Those who criticize unity forms have no plan of their own. They don't want to talk to brothers with whom they differ. And they don't want you talking to them either. Our greatest hindrance to real power and growth is ourselves. As Pogo says, "We has met the enemy and he is us!" We've shot ourselves in the foot. We must heal! And get on with it! If the challenges facing us are met!

### *WHAT DO WE NEED TO DO?*

When God sends a criticism He also sends a solution. Ephesus was to do three things. We must do the same!
*Remember* (vs. 5)! They were to remember the "height from which they had fallen"! Ephesus knew what it was to stand on the mountain. So, I say, do we! We know what it is to be saved by the grace of God and the gospel of Christ. Every church has surely seen God in action changing the lives

100

of men and women. They've seen sinners won from the pit of hell. They've known revivals, answered prayer and the indwelling Holy Spirit. We've got to remember all this. Don't settle for anything less than this! We must remember the gospel is "good news"! Let's quit using our pulpits for telling what's wrong in the world and in the church. Let's give hurting and lost people hope through Jesus Christ. Let's remember to fight the devil not each other. Let's remember our mission, to "seek and save the lost" (Luke 19:10).

*Repent* (vs. 5)! This was the call to five of the seven churches of Asia (Rev. 2,3). I wonder if the ratio is not the same today? Jesus said, "Repent or perish" (Luke 13:3)! Someone said, "What we need today are more Nathans saying to sinful Davids, 'Thou art the man'!" But there's too much David in our Nathans. As in Israel's defeats God' people have too much "sin in the camp" (Josh. 7:11). We've called the world to "repent and be baptized" (Acts 2:38). It is time for the people of God to repent of their sins also. There is no sin in the world that is not also flourishing in the church. We must repent! We must repent of our apathy, our ritualism and judgmentalism. We must repent of our selfishness and fruitlessness. We must repent of hiding and hoarding the gospel of Christ from those who need it so badly.

*Return* (vs. 5)! "Do the things you did at first!" John said they had left their "first love." Do you remember your first love? Your first kiss? Your noses probably bumped. Where do you put your nose anyway when you kiss? It was all fumbly but my what excitement. That's the way it was when we were new Christians. It was exciting. It was exhilarating! There's nothing like the zeal and excitement of new converts. But in marriages and in churches things can go stale. The weddings bells go from clink to clank to clunk! You start taking things for granted. Marriage goes from bliss to blah! And church can be the same way.

It's time to return! We should never get over glory! Praise

God there's something to which to return! There's a Jesus Who loves us. There's a Holy Spirit to indwell us. To lead and guide us! There's the church family. What a fellowship! What a joy divine! Nothing is more boring than a church service if the relationship with the Lord has been lost. Nothing is more electrifying when saints come together where God, Christ, the Holy Spirit and the gospel are fresh in our souls.

## THESE BLESSINGS AWAIT US!

You can keep your golden lampstand (Rev. 2:5)! Their lampstand of identity was threatened by their fall. It is therefore guaranteed by their return. We can be identified as the people of God. There is no greater distinction or blessing than to be God's children and know it!

You'll eat of the tree of life (vs. 7). All this means is that you'll partake of what really gives life. Both now and in eternity. Christians really live! Jesus promises "life to the full" (John 10:10). Yes, what the world wants to see is the real thing. And if it is shown to people entering the exciting twenty-first century spectacular things will happen. I want in on that. How about you?

# 13

## TALKING "TO" EACH OTHER, NOT "ABOUT" EACH OTHER!

It was my second scheduled trip to the little south Texas town. It was a small church and they hoped I would say something to boost them toward love and good works. I had been there before. They had a good attitude. My first visit seemed to do them good. They asked for more. I had enjoyed the previous trip. I was looking forward to being with them again.

Then came the call from the elders. Someone in the area (from a neighboring church) raised some objection about my being there. They had four criticisms about what they had heard I believed and taught. Were these things true? The local elders were good men, and just trying to do their job. I assured them the accusations weren't true. Well then, would I come anyway, and meet with the accuser? Yes, of course I would! But the man leveling the criticism didn't want to meet with me. On insistence from the elders he reluctantly came, bringing a friend along to help. The meeting was conducted after the service on my first night there.

The elders did a good job. They read the accusations and asked that I respond to them. I reassured them I did not believe or practice as accused. The accuser was very uncomfortable. "I've read articles written by others about you. I know what you believe!" I said, "Now you're hearing from my own mouth what I teach. I do not believe and preach those things! I'm either telling you the truth or lying! What do you think it is?" And this brother said, "I believe you're lying!" I wish this was only an isolated example!

"The rumor spread" (John 21:23). Upon receiving his marching orders from Jesus, Peter said, "Well what about him (John)?" And Jesus said, "If I want him to remain alive until I return, what is that to you?" And the rumor spread among the disciples that John would not die! Scripture plainly says, "But Jesus did not say that he would not die; he only said, 'If I want him to remain alive until I return, what is that to you?' " Times haven't changed.

I wish I had a dollar for every rumor I've heard about the Garnett church where I have ministered for twenty years. It has been rumored that these have all preached in our pulpit: Oral Roberts, Mayor Robert LaFortune, Senator David Boren and others. Did they? No! Then where did the rumors come from? God alone knows!

Rumors have circulated about my own ministry and life. When invited to speak on the Abilene Christian University's lectureship, a fellow wrote those in charge that they should know that I was no longer preaching at Garnett, that I had resigned and was now teaching in an instrumental college in Kentucky. Not true! Other rumors have included that I have quit preaching, been fired, left Garnett, left the church, divorced my wife, married again and that I died of a heart attack! I feel like Mark Twain who said, "Rumors of my death have been greatly exaggerated!"

So much damage is done by unfounded rumors. And if the teller of tales should be hanged by the tongue, then perhaps the hearer should be hanged by the ears. Some of these rumors are funny. Others are serious. And damage could be avoided if people realized the object of the rumor probably has a telephone and a mail box!

## *LOOSE TALK IS A SIN!*

No other sin is more soundly thrashed in scripture. Take time for a deeper look at the following verses:

"Slanderers will not inherit the kingdom of God" (I Cor. 6:10).
"Quarreling, jealousy, outbursts of anger, factions, slander, gossip, arrogance and disorder" (II Cor. 12:20)
"Discord, jealousy, selfish ambition, dissensions, factions" (Gal. 5:19,20)
"Falsehood . . . unwholesome talk" (Eph. 4:25,29)
"Slander, filthy language, lies" (Col. 3:8,9)
"Slanderous" (II Tim. 3:3)
"A busybody in other men's matters" (I Pet. 4:16, KJV)
"Liars" (Rev. 21:8).

And please note the company these sins are in. Right alongside of adultery, murder, stealing and the like. God takes a pretty dim view of how we treat one another.

The book of James (chapter three) does a real treatise on sins of the tongue!

He tells us,

"the tongue is like a bit in a horse's mouth" vs. 3
"like a rudder on a ship" vs. 4
"can harm like a raging forest fire" vs. 5
"a world of evil corrupting the whole person" vs. 6
"a restless evil full of deadly poison" vs. 7,8
"can even be used to curse God" v. 9

## WHAT THE BIBLE SAYS ABOUT LOOSE TALK!

Therefore if you are offering your gift before the altar and there remember that your brother has something against you, leave your gift there in front of the altar. First go and be reconciled to your brother; then come and offer your gift. (Matt. 5:23,24)

It is sad to see brethren scrambling for excuses rather than just doing what the Lord commands. "That was before the Christian age!" "Well he didn't sin against me personally!" These are really cop-outs to keep from settling things the Lord's way.

Again,

If your brother sins against you, go and show him his fault, just between the two of you. If he listens to you, you have won your brother over. But if he will not listen, take one or two others along, so that every matter may be established by the testimony of two or three witnesses. If he refuses to listen to them, tell it to the church; and if he refuses to listen even to the church, treat him as you would a pagan or a tax collector. (Matt. 18:15-18)

There are four steps in this process:
(1) Settle the matter between the two of you!
(2) Take one or two witnesses!
(3) Tell it to the church!
(4) Withdrawal of fellowship!

Each time the aim is to settle the matter with as few involved as possible. For shame that our brotherhood wants to air our dirty linen to the world. And that without proven facts or even first contacting the brother in question!

## THE NASHVILLE AGREEMENT!

Some years ago a young brother in the Nashville area

called me. "Marvin, how do you handle a brother who is always against everything we do? He's against every speaker we invite and against every program we try to start. He's got all sorts of accusations he's heard and rumors he's believed. He stops every good work we want to start!" Well, since he had also been opposed to my coming to that church I suggested they handle it in the following way. Tell the brother you are concerned about his accusation. Appoint a night when he can meet with the elders and talk to the accused. In my case that took a conference call. It went something like this.

"Marvin, this is John Doe. I'm one of the elders at Blank St. church. All the elders are here in this room, and two of our members. Is it all right if we ask about a few things that need clarification?"

I assured him it was. They brought up the accusations. I answered them as clearly and briefly as I could. They gave the accuser a chance to ask me anything he wanted. He brought up what he'd read about me in a certain brotherhood journal. I answered. The chairman of the elders then said, "Marvin, thanks for your time. Your answers have been clear. We are satisfied. Now we need to hang up because we have some work to do!"

Then hung up. They called upon the brother to repent. They gave him two weeks to do so before the whole church. When he refused they marked him publicly according to Romans 16:17! I heartily propose this procedure as being both scriptural and effective. Snipers will continue to shoot at God's leaders until this method brings the matter to a close!

## BRETHREN DISCUSSING THEIR DIFFERENCES!

Churches of Christ have always been willing to debate their cause. The first fifty years of this century were characterized by debates all over the nation. There was the famous Campbell-Owen (Atheist) Debate. There were debates with every denominational preacher we could stir up. Debates over baptism, falling from grace, the Holy Spirit, speaking in tongues and many other subjects. When we ran out of denominational preachers to debate, we turned on each other. We debated the "one-cuppers," "anti-class brethren" and the "non-institutional brethren." We debated instrumental music in Christian worship. Some of these discussions were no doubt good. Many were "dog fights" to say the least! The danger of the formal debate was that each side sent in their champion whose desire was to "search and destroy." It seemed we really did not know how to discuss differences in any framework except this.

But many brethren loved each other, yet seriously disagreed over various issues. Some longed for a forum for open discussion, free exchange of ideas in an atmosphere of study, mutual respect and prayer. It is surprising to say the least that there would be so much opposition to this! Many church bulletins and brotherhood periodicals openly blasted the other side, but steadfastly refused to sit at the discussion table with them. And they criticized those who would!

### ONE BODY!

I've been a regular writer for a publication called "One Body"! It is published by Don DeWelt, an instrumental brother in Joplin, Missouri. This well-respected brother has a passion for fair and open discussion. He began this paper as a forum for "any brother who has anything constructive to say about how we might get together"! There are no strings attached. Anyone may write his convictions and concerns. All brother DeWelt asks is that you do it in a spirit of love (Eph. 4:15). I have been amazed at those who not only would not write for this paper, but would brand those who would as "selling out the faith." Hard, indeed, to understand! I recommend the paper. And it is still open to all writers under the same conditions!

## RESTORATION FORUMS

We've alluded to the Restoration Forums in this book! There have been seven of them to date. That is, on a national scale. There have been many more across the nation. Again it is amazing to read some of the criticisms of these forums. All can attend. Most anyone can speak. And they are far from being meetings of compromise and agreement not to deal with our differences. Great discussions on instrumental music in worship, the silence of the scriptures, Hermeneutics, fellowship, consistency and other matters have been openly and frankly discussed. I heartily recommend these annual forums. Send your preachers and elders to them. Attend yourself. I am committed to this type of frank, brotherly discussion of our differences. One thing will come across loud and clear. The things on which we agree far outweigh the things about which we disagree. We've talked about each other long enough. Now let's get in on the marvelous practice of talking *to* each other. If we're going to heaven together, it just might be nice to get acquainted before we make the trip!

# 14

## PAPERS, PARTIES AND PREJUDICE!

It was a long flight home. Two long legs of the journey from Alaska to Tulsa, Oklahoma. The 2:05 a.m. flight out of Anchorage puts you in Salt Lake City, Utah at 8:45 a.m. Then a long layover before the four and one half hours on to Tulsa. What do you do with time on your hands and nothing to do?

Newsstands offer everything imaginable. Newspapers from all over the world. New York Times. Dallas Morning News. Even the Tulsa World. Magazines like Time, Newsweek, US News and World Report cover everything from the San Francisco earthquake to the Berlin Wall. From there it branches out to Homes, Fashion and Sports. There is a selection of the ever-popular self-help books featuring Zig Ziglar and Dale Carnegie. Religious books are there too, authored by such familiar names as Schuller, Peale, Dobson and Swindoll. From there it deteriorates by way of National Enquirer, Playboy and the cheap soft back porn.

## THE PRINTED PAGE AMONG US!

It's about the same kind of selection available to church of Christ members. Really good, helpful stuff from the pen of Rubel Shelly and Max Lucado. Brotherhood periodicals, mostly good, thought provoking articles by prominent men and women of our brotherhood. From there we go to the weekly church bulletins around the country. And finally we have our own "National Enquirers." "Yellow journalism" as it has been dubbed. So called because it deals in articles calculated to expose some church or preacher as "liberal" or simply a "false teacher"!

Not that it is wrong to point out error, but beware of any publication that majors in finger pointing. We're usually "down on" what we're not "up on"! And if editors have smut on their minds, many readers have vacuum cleaner minds; you know, always picking up dirt!

What brotherhood papers do you take? It is an often asked question! Long ago I quit taking any paper just because it was written by some brother. I need all the help I can get! I simply cannot take a diet that is all "against." I have enough doubts of my own; tell me something you believe in!

I came up with three rules for writing (or reading). (1) Does it draw you closer to Jesus? (2) Does it bring out the best in you? (3) Does it serve any useful purpose? I suggest it would be best for you to abide by these three rules of reading or writing!

"As a man thinks in his heart, so is he" (Prov. 23:7)! Or as positive thinking speakers put it, "Your life becomes what your mind is fed!" G.I.G.O.! "Garbage in; garbage out!" You can become just about anything you want to become. But you're going to have to feed your mind properly. You can't afford too much garbage in your minds. To be sure there are good biscuits in garbage cans. But you'll have to eat a lot of bad stuff before you get to it. Be careful what you read!

People ask me, "Did you read that article against you in the "Blank Publication" (name withheld intentionally!)? No! Oh, I'm curious all right. But it ruins my attitude. It brings out the worst in me. I want to respond in kind. It wasn't Christlike of the writer. And it doesn't make me respond in a Christlike manner. So if he doesn't stop writing like that, at least I can stop reading what he writes. Some day we'll catch on that yellow journalism demands a market. When the market disappears the publication will cease.

## THE PARTISAN SPIRIT AMONG US!

The publications among us have been responsible for the splits, division, separation and sectarian spirit between brethren. Brethren have a tendency to line up behind certain papers, causing the party spirit.

Someone has said, "In ecumenical movements it takes preachers to hold them together; in restoration churches, it takes preachers to keep us apart!" You've heard of large mergers of several denominations? The people don't ask to get together. Their preachers meet in conventions and vote to merge them into a super denomination. Members don't like this. Their delegates vote them in against their will. I am convinced it is preachers and papers that keep the people of God apart. All baptized believers have been added to one Family. There are differences and difficulties of course. But by and large they long to be together and to fellowship one another. "How good and pleasant it is when brethren dwell together in unity" (Psa. 133:1)! But differences are exaggerated and distorted through the pens of unscrupulous editors and in the pulpits of sectarian preachers. In many cases these are men who do not check the facts, have not met with the people they attack. And usually they are not up on the issues they hold as walls between!

Many brethren's convictions are not based on the Bible but upon the stand of some preacher or periodical. "The 'such and such church' or 'that preacher' must be a bad apple. I read about him in my church paper. My editor said it was so; so it must be so!" Like as not that editor has never met with the brother he castigates. The object of his assassination has never been phoned, written or contacted in any way! Yet thousands read and believe without investigation.

Editors have a tremendous power. And it can be used for either good or bad. Unfortunately many misuse that power. Character is assassinated. Walls of separation are created. No good purpose is served. Lots of damage!

## OUR PREJUDICES!

Unfortunately it is easier to believe the bad than the good. If you hear that John was seen coming out of a night club you respond, "I always suspected John had a drinking problem!" But if you hear Mary inherited a million dollars and is in Acapulco on vacation you say, "No, you're kidding!?" And some don't seem to want the truth. They just want to be the one to pass along the rumor.

I got a phone call from a Harding College student. While at home his preacher had publicly stated a falsehood about me. He called to see if it was true. It was not! I wrote the preacher. "Dear brother. It was reported you accused me of this. It is not true. Here is the truth. I know you want the truth, so I'll hope to hear that you have corrected your mistake." No answer! Three letters later I sent a copy to his elders. They called him in and demanded that he correct his error. He refused. They fired him. Then he wrote the Garnett elders accusing me of being a troublemaker and getting him fired. Isn't life strange?

Prejudice causes us to do strange things. Brethren will demand that you believe every issue just exactly as they do. They demand further that you draw lines of fellowship where they do. They demand that you not fellowship brethren they have decided not to fellowship. Then they climax this by threatening spiritual assassination if you don't comply. It is simply asking too much. I'm going to love all the Family. I will discuss differences with anyone, but I will fellowship my brethren.

And I will preach anywhere I feel I can be of use to the cause of Christ. Preachers are sometimes heavily criticized for preaching among brethren with whom we disagree. This is especially true when non-instrumental preachers preach in instrumental churches.

Jesus drew heavy criticism for his association with the "wrong crowd." His answer was, "It is not the healthy who need a doctor but the sick" (Matt. 9:12)! The apostles preached in Jewish synagogues, in the marketplace, in front of idols, before the Romans, even in prison. If anything, we have more authority to preach among sinners than among the righteous!

But some brethren say, "Yes, but they are 'erring brethren'!" And I say with all kindness, "I didn't know there were any other kind!" I ask humbly that you judge me by *what* I say, not *where* I say it!

We've got to have some courageous preachers. Men who are not afraid of losing their jobs. Men who are not afraid of their peers or the brotherhood mafia. Men who will love God and the truth first; then will love the whole family of God. Men who will even love their critics. But who will not allow critics to dominate and manipulate them into sterility!


## AN APPEAL FOR "WHOLESOME WORDS"!

I heard the television evangelist say, "Denominations

are not what is bad. *Denominationalism* is what's bad!" I did a double-take. Then I realized what he was really saying. It isn't *difference* but *divisiveness* that the Bible condemns. Take a closer look at Romans 16:17:

> I urge you, brothers, to watch out for those who cause divisions and put obstacles in your way that are contrary to the teaching you have learned. Keep away from them!

Not every difference is divisive. Brethren hold all kinds of opinions on non-essential things but do not cause division over them. Let us be careful in our honest convictions that we are true to the book but not divisive when we don't get our way!

And my last appeal in this chapter:

> Do not let any unwholesome talk come out of your mouths, but only what is helpful for building others up according to their needs, that it may benefit those who listen. (Eph. 4:29)

Editors, authors and preachers, let's watch what we write and preach. Preach the Word! But don't misuse your great power of influence to divide brethren over non-essential things. Let's be body builders, not body destroyers. The pen is mightier than the sword. And the soul you save may very well be your own!

# 15

## BY THIS SHALL ALL MEN KNOW!

A new comandment I give unto you, That ye love one another; as I have loved you, that ye also love one another. By this shall all men know that ye are my disciples, if ye have love one to another! (John 13:34,35, KJV)

"What is so rare as a day in June?" Maybe a day when brethren in Restoration Churches can disagree and still demonstrate a sweet, loving spirit toward one another!

### THE CARTOON THAT INSPIRED THIS BOOK!

I still remember the day I saw it! Funny looking cartoon. Back view of one man holding a shot gun. Facing a fellow looking back at him over a nose-high fence. All that was showing was this guy's face, nose and fingers exposed to the man with the gun. And the caption, "Don't shoot! We may both be on the same side!"

And I thought, "How typical!" There's a lot of fighting among the people of God. Some religious fighting is necessary of course. The shield of faith and the sword of the Spirit are weapons of war. But these were to be turned on the enemy not against one another. Saddest of all are the fights between brothers in the Family of God. Brothers who equally love God and reverence the inspiration and authority of His word.

Just here I think it would be good to let our "fingers do the walking through the yellow pages" of the New Testament on these beautiful but too infrequently practiced verses:

Have sincere love for your brothers. (I Pet. 1:22)

Now about brotherly love, we do not need to write you, for you, yourselves have been taught by God to love each other. And in fact, you do love all the brothers throughout Macedonia. Yet we urge you, brothers, to do so more and more. (I Thess. 4:9,10)

Love must be sincere. Hate what is evil; cling to what is good. Be devoted to one another in brotherly love. (Rom. 12:9,10)

Love always protects, always trusts, always hopes, always perseveres. Love never fails. (I Cor. 13:7,8)

Keep on loving each other as brothers. (Heb. 13:1)

Anyone who claims to be in the light but hates his brother is still in the darkness. Whoever loves his brother lives in the light! (I John 2:9,10)

Dear friends, let us love one another, for love comes from God. Everyone who loves has been born of God and knows God. Whoever does not love, does not know God, because God is love. . . . Dear Friends, since God so loved us we also ought to love one another. No one has ever seen God; but if we love each other, God lives in us and his love is made complete in us. (I John 4:8,11,12)

Love the brotherhood of believers. (I Pet. 2:17)

## LOVE IS THE "MISSING INGREDIENT"!

Love is at least as important as baptism, the Lord's supper and giving! After all Jesus did *not* say "By acapella singing all will know you are my disciples"! Neither did He single out weekly observance of communion or the sign in front of our buildings as these identifying marks. Since it was "by *this* shall all men know you are my disciples, *that you love one another*," maybe we ought to take another look at how we treat one another!

Have you paid close attention to the way we treat one another when we disagree? Brethren can be downright vicious toward one another. We can be merciless in debating. Some seem to enjoy writing some brother up or spreading unkind rumors! Common courtesies extended to strangers are not extended toward a brother with whom we disagree.

I got a phone call. "I hear you are having Joe Smith (not his real name) speak on the Tulsa workshop this year!" I assured him we had invited brother Smith to speak. "Do you know how he stands on divorce and remarriage?" he asked. I admitted I didn't. I further told this brother his stand on divorce and remarriage was not the issue when we extended our invitation for that brother to speak. I said we'd invited brother Smith to speak because he loved the Lord, believed in Bible authority, was a faithful gospel preacher and a soul-winner. The brother insisted because of that brother's stand on the divorce question he should not be used in any capacity. Dear friends such thinking is unacceptable. Surely you know if we selected only those speakers who agree with us on every issue we couldn't put on a workshop at all! Let's be more charitable than this with each other.

## LOVE BOTH "LIBERALS" AND "CONSERVATIVES"

It is sometimes easier to reach out to those more liberal than we than to those more conservative! It is harder to love those who criticize us, write unkind articles about us and slander us to the thousands of readers of a particular publication! Yet these are included in Jesus' words to "love one another." Jesus Himself was faced with loving the unlovable. And did so admirably!

I once spoke to a famous television evangelist. He said, "You're not the typical church of Christ preacher I've met!" Whatever that meant, he then said, "I imagine you get a lot of criticism!" I admitted that I get "my share" (?). He then gave me something to really think about. He said, "Pick out the man or the publication that criticizes you the most. How do you feel about him? That's the real test to see if you have the spirit of Christ in you!" Ouch!

You see, sometimes I want to step softly outside my circle of Christianity, sock my critic in the teeth, and then step comfortably back inside that circle! That's how far I am from looking like Jesus. When I see the way Jesus responded to those who slapped Him and spat in His face I am drawn to respond more like my Lord! Oh God, let us love one another even when treated unfairly!

## "THE IMPORTANT THING!"

It was visiting day at the Roman prison. Brethren came to see Paul. They told him he was getting unfavorable publicity by those who filled the pulpit in his absence. It wasn't fair!

What can we do to stop them? Paul gave an unexpected answer. "What does it matter? The important thing is Christ is preached. And because of this I rejoice" (Phil. 1:18). Some things are just more important than other things. Paul expressed this attitude in other writings. "The only thing that counts is faith expressing itself through love" (Gal. 5:6). Peter adds, "Above all, love each other deeply, because love covers over a multitude of sins." He is not saying love is a substitute for obedience. But he does give us the solid teaching that when you get love on straight, your intention makes up for a lot of human error. And praise God for that!

So which is more important? Accuracy or intention? Rightness in law or real love for the Lawgiver? The following verses will help.

> These people honor me with their lips, but their hearts are far from me. They worship me in vain; their teachings are but rules taught by men. (Matt. 15:8,9).

I suggest reading verses one through nine. Jesus is concerned both by our hearts (intention) and His teaching (doctrine). The Pharisees had been so concerned with being right doctrinally. But their hearts weren't right. This made their worship worthless! In the matter of doctrine and heart there are only four possibilities for all of us:

1. Right in doctrine; right in heart!
2. Right in doctrine; wrong in heart!
3. Wrong in doctrine; wrong in heart!
4. Wrong (mistaken) in doctrine; right in heart (intention)!

Naturally number one is the ideal. And it is that for which we must all strive. God will accept no less than this! But while we may all be right in heart, is there one among us who claims to be 100% right on all doctrinal points?

Position two was where the Pharisees were. Legalistically

right in doctrine; but wrong in heart. And Jesus said their worship was worthless!

Position three won't get it either! Heart not right; doctrine not right either!

Our only hope is in position four. Attitude toward God and His Word right. We really want to honor Him and follow His Word accurately. But our humanity catches up with us! In our best efforts we err in so many ways! So our only chance of being saved is that God will see our genuine desire to please Him and follow His word. And that His grace will cover human error.

God must extend His amazing grace to save us! Why is it so difficult to extend it to one another? Are we afraid to assume someone is "saved" with whom we have a serious doctrinal disagreement? Then let's get out of the judging business altogether. Let's leave it to the only One qualified in the first place!


## LET'S RESTORE THAT GOOD OLD FAMILY FEELING!

I heard a television preacher telling about a "vision" he'd had! He saw an old man crying uncontrollably. When asked why he was crying he replied, "We have a little three year old girl in our family. She's blind. The other children put things in her path so she'll stumble over them. They lead her to walk off the porch. And they laugh at the expense of their little sister. And we have a six year old retarded son. They laugh at the way he walks and talks. They call him names. They invite neighborhood children over to make sport of their retarded brother. We also have a teenage daughter. She got in with the wrong crowd. She got pregnant and she's not married. The children have told everyone at school and their sister is publicly disgraced." And then the old man (God) added, "That's my church. And I'm brokenhearted at the way my children treat each other!"

Members of my family have their faults. We can talk about them but you cannot! I'm so defensive when it comes to members of my immediate family. Let's start thinking of all baptized believers as being in the Family of God with us. They can be wrong. They can be lost. But let's always treat them as loving members of the Family. Jesus said it is the only thing the world can see that would identify us as the family of God!

# 16

## THAT THE WORLD MAY BELIEVE!

My prayer is not for them alone. I pray also for those who will believe in me through their message, that all of them may be one, Father, just as you are in me and I am in you. May they also be in us so that the world may believe that you have sent me! (John 17:20,21)

Gethsemane. Deep in prayer. Anguished in spirit. Heart breaking. Overwhelmed in spirit. Three disciples. Keep watch with me. Tired. Asleep. Father! If possible! Let this cup pass. Not My will but Your will be done! I pray for My people. Let them be one. The world will believe if they are one! Let them be one like Us. Let them be one *for* Us! Please Father, don't let them get sidetracked. Don't let Satan divide them!

When Jesus finished praying He found the disciples sleeping. Blissfully unaware of three earth shattering matters of importance:

(1) That it was only hours before Jesus would die a horrible death on the cross!
(2) That the salvation of the world hinged on the old rugged cross!
(3) That the difference in salvation and damnation would depend largely on the unity of Christ's followers!

Ahead was the cross. Cruel trial. Stripped and flogged. Crown of thorns. Spit. Nails. Pain. My God why have you forsaken me? It is finished! Death! Darkness! Peace!

Two thousand years later. And the disciples of Jesus are still largely asleep. Oblivious to the prayer of Jesus. Unmoved by the Savior's last request, "Let them all be one"! Lost in our sectarian orthodoxy is the reasoning of Jesus that the world won't be *won* unless we are *one*! One last glance backward at the cross. If Jesus would do all that to save a lost world, can we afford to do less?

### JESUS WANTED A WORLD SAVED!

We are told that

> Nothing in all creation is hidden from God's sight. Everything is uncovered and laid bare before the eyes of him to whom we must give account. (Heb. 4:13)

Our world has been bathed in sin from Day One. God has seen it all. He watched the rebellion of His first two humans. By the time of Noah God had seen man's great wickedness, and that "every inclination of the thoughts of his heart was only evil all the time" (Gen. 6:5). A black line of sin runs through the whole Bible and spills out into the twentieth century.

And wonder of wonders! God saw it all. And still thought man was worth saving. So,

> God so loved the world that he gave his one and only Son,

126

that whoever believes in him shall not perish but have eternal life. (John 3:16)

The cross says two things loud and clear. It tells how bad sin is. Your sin is so bad it took the death of Jesus on the cross to buy your redemption. But the cross also tells how valuable you are; worth the death of Jesus on the cross. He was willing to go that far that you and I might be saved. And God is not willing that anyone be lost (II Pet. 3:9).

What did He see in them? What does He see in us today? Whatever it is I wish we could see it in each other! Love brought the Christ. Christ brought the gospel. The gospel brought the opportunity. And it will take the unity of believers to bring the plan to fulfillment; the belief of an unbelieving world. The difference in salvation and damnation will be the oneness of the disciples of Jesus.

Jesus said it would take the unity of believers to bring the world to faith in Jesus Christ. What, then, would be Satan's most powerful tool against world evangelism? Would it not be the sad spectacle of religious division we see in today's world? Where, then, are your own efforts, desires and prayers? I suggest that we would all fit into one of the following categories:

(1) Apathetic about the unity of God's people, and therefore about world evangelism!
(2) Downright against it! Refusal to fellowship others unless they totally surrender to all our quirks, whims, opinions and conclusions!
(3) Wishing it would happen, but doing nothing !
(4) Actively pursuing unity at all costs except at the expense of essential truth!

*WE LIVE IN AN UNBELIEVING WORLD!*

The early church practiced unity. They got together with

God! They got together with each other. They fit into the plan of God. And within thirty years they preached the gospel "to every creature under heaven" (Col. 1:23).

It is now two thousand years since that first gospel sermon on Pentecost morning. How are we doing? There's only one word for it. Poorly! There isn't a nation, a city or a single congregation that is really making an impact for Christ! Christianity in its broadest definition isn't a drop in the bucket when compared with eastern religions. There are yet whole nations where Jesus Christ is not actively preached.

Then we turn to America. One nation under God! A nation formed for "freedom of worship." A nation where once all its leaders were highly religious men with a deep and abiding faith in Jesus Christ and His Word. A nation where prayer was a vital part in every meeting of its highest leaders. A nation whose constitution and bill of rights were written from the Bible! Is America a "believing nation" today?

I suggest that of two hundred fifty million Americans who are alive today, over eighty million of them claim to be atheists. Another fifteen million are practicing Jews who deny that Jesus Christ is the Messiah. The modern church is so divided that it is all but drained completely of its power. A field for evangelism rather than a force for evangelism. While the world goes to hell because of unbelief, the modern church is "navel gazing"! It concerns itself with irrelevent issues. It disdains efforts to restore the unity for which Jesus prayed. It assassinates its own who attempt to bridge the chasms between us. And the situation will not change until the people of God give fresh attention to the prayer of Jesus for the unity of His people!

## WHY DOES THE WORLD NOT BELIEVE?

Three answers may be given. (1) Immorality! We may

reason that people would rather sin than believe. And we'd have scripture for this. "This is the verdict; Light has come into the world, but men loved darkness instead of light because their deeds were evil" (John 3:19). (2) Communism! Basically God denying. Where communism reigns religion fades. Churches are closed! Belief is ridiculed! Karl Marx called religion "the opiate of the people"! (3) False Religions! That is pagan religions such as Hindu, Moslem, even Satanism.

The above three things are definitely against God. But Jesus did not list any of them as being obstacles of belief. Jesus maintained that when His people are one, "the world will believe"! No power can compete with God (Rom. 8:31)! No message is as explosive as the gospel (Rom. 1:16)! Nothing can successfully come against God and His truth. Nothing, that is, except the division of God's own people! It's no wonder Paul wrote, "Mark them that cause division" (Rom. 16:17). Divisive people (not just "different" people) do untold harm to the cause of world evangelism. It is Satan's greatest weapon with which to defeat the prayer of Jesus. The temple of truth has not been harmed by woodpeckers on the outside as much as by termites on the inside. The church of Christ has shot itself in the foot. And we limp on our mission in a jet age world! We are like a bicycle chasing a jet airplane. We're both going in the same direction, but that's where the comparison ends. The solution to the problem is the unity of God's people. Just like Jesus prayed!

## OBSTACLES TO UNITY!

I want to suggest six things that stand in the way of unity among God's people.

1. Truth! The only thing worse than division is unity with error! Error, that is, on essential matters. There can be no unity with people who oppose the Lordship of Jesus and the

authority of His Word. The truth will set you free (John 8:32). But it will also separate between those who will accept it.

2. Opinion made into law! There are many things we have liberty to decide for ourselves. We do not all have to believe and practice alike. A study of Romans, chapters fourteen and fifteen is important. Religious days and foods are given as examples. "Each one should be fully convinced in his own mind" (Rom. 14:5). We own freedom of choice in these areas. But we may not bind our opinions on others.

3. Tradition made equal to law! "You nullify the word of God for sake of your tradition" (Matt. 15:6). This one is similar to number two. I list it separate because when an opinion item is practiced for a long period of time it gains "law" status. Now what we've done for many years becomes "God's law." Since customs and cultures vary in different parts of the world, tradition becomes an impossible base upon which to build unity.

4. Arrogance! Diotrephes (III John vs. 9,10)! He loved "to be first." He wanted to call the shots. It was rule or ruin. It may be a preacher or elder. But when human beings insist on being followed, division and disaster follow. All Christians are slaves to Christ. We take the best slaves and appoint them our elders and ministers! There will be no unity while men play King of the Mountain!

5. Apathy! One man was asked, "Do you think ignorance or apathy is the biggest problem in the church today?" His reply? "I don't know and I don't care!" Why do believers remain isolated from each other? We just don't care enough to do something about it. I praise God for these modern day saints who don't claim to have all the answers but who care enough to try. Sometimes at great cost!

6. Last of all I suggest, procrastination! There are many good people of God who know division is not right. They are concerned about the prayer of Jesus, the unity of the brethren and the salvation of the world. And in there somewhere are

some plans to attempt reconciliation. They're going to meet the preacher from that other church. They will set up some sort of forum for prayerful discussion. Someday! But "someday" is not on any calendar. The "convenient season" for which we look never comes.

Let's get serious about the prayer of Jesus! And about bringing an unbelieving world to faith in our Lord. Let's pray more about unity. Let's take overt action to talk with those with whom we differ (individuals and churches)! The world will be brought to Christ to the degree that we are successful in bringing brother to brother. You may have been part of the problem. It's so much more exciting to be part of the solution!

# 17

## BOWLING BALLS AND BULL'S-EYES!

Teacher, which is the greatest commandment in the law?
(Matt. 22:36)

Are the commands of God more like bowling or archery?
In bowling all the pins count the same. No matter the position. The important thing is how many you can knock down.
They are all totaled up. That's your score!

In archery you aim at the bull's-eye! The closer you get to
the bull's-eye the higher you score. Which illustration fits the
commands of God? If bowling, then performance is all that
counts. If archery, a steady aim for dead center is what's important!

Let's take a closer look at a verse that has troubled us.

For whoever keeps the whole law and yet stumbles at just one
point is guilty of breaking all of it. (James 2:10)

133

If God uses the bowling method to judge us we are ruined. We try so hard to understand and do all God wants. But we mess up on just one point and wham, we are guilty of breaking the whole law. Unless you can score one hundred percent you can't be saved. Don't you hope this isn't what that verse meant? But if not, just what does it mean?

James is teaching that you may not "cafeteria" the law of God. When going through a cafeteria line you select some of this and some of that. You pass right by certain items and take only small portions of others. You may not do this with the will of God! You may not say to God, "I'll keep ninety percent of your law. But there's ten percent I just won't do!" Rebellion on any part of the law of God will result in your condemnation as a "lawbreaker!"

## THE LAW OF GOD IS IMPORTANT!

God wanted what He wrote; and He wrote what He wanted! All scripture is "God-breathed" (II Tim. 3:16). Jesus said those who reject His words would be condemned at the last day (John 12:48). John's picture of the judgment is graphic. Your life will be placed on one side of God's balance scales, His Word on the other. And "the dead were judged according to what they had done as recorded in the books" (Rev. 20:12,13). There is no substitute for obedience (cf. Matt. 7:21; Heb. 5:8,9).

## BUT GOD HAS AN "EMPHASIS!"

God has a "bull's-eye." And He demands that we aim for it. Nothing short of that aim will save. It is time we find out what it is and dedicate our lives to that sharp aim.

Jesus gave a scathing denunciation to the Pharisees. They

were so careful to measure out an exact tithe to God. Right down to their garden spices — mint, dill and cummin. But they had neglected the "more important matters of the law" — justice, mercy and faithfulness (Matt. 23:23,24). He called them hypocrites, blind guides who would strain out a gnat but swallow a camel. Interesting!

Two chapters later (Matt. 25:31-46) Jesus treated the very subject of how we will be judged for eternity. He claims all men will one day stand before God. They will be divided into two classes. Those on the right from those on the left. The sheep from the goats. The saved from the lost. And what separated them for eternity? Their treatment of their fellowman. I was hungry and you fed me. I was thirsty and you gave me a drink. I was a stranger and you showed hospitality. I was naked and you gave me clothes. I was in prison and you ministered to me!

Paul tells us what is of "first importance," that "Christ died for our sins according to the Scriptures, that he was buried, that he was raised on the third day according to the Scriptures" (I Cor. 15:1-3).

In a previous chapter we called attention to this emphasis of Scripture. "By *this* will all men know you are my disciples" (John 13:35). "The only thing that counts" (Gal. 5:6). "The important thing is" (Phil. 1:18). "Above all else" (I Pet. 4:8).

We now take a broader look at the text of this chapter.

One of them, an expert in the law, tested him with this question:'Teacher, which is the greatest commandment in the Law?' Jesus replied, 'Love the Lord your God with all your heart and with all your soul and with all your mind.' This is the *first and greatest commandment*. And the second is like it; 'Love your neighbor as yourself.' All the Law and the Prophets hang on these commandments. (Matt. 22:35-41)

We are trying to show that God has an emphasis. A bull's-eye. And what is that bull's-eye? From the verses above

135

we conclude the emphasis of God is "justice, mercy, faithfulness, loving service to our fellowman, preaching and accepting the death, burial and resurrection of Jesus. And loving God with all our hearts!

That's what God counts! What do we count? Things like budget, buses and buildings; carpet, cooling and committees. We count attendance, number of baptisms and programs. Now all these things are important. But they are clearly not on the "emphasis" list of God.

We sometimes focus on the periphery of the target. Sometimes our attention, energies, time and money are spent on things not on the target at all. There is too little emphasis on the bull's-eye itself: that of loving Jesus and leading lost people to Him.

I remember speaking in a little Oklahoma town. It was one of those meetings where they had a different speaker every night. My assigned topic was "The Mission of the Church." The song leader told the audience, "I don't know which mission he'll speak on. We'll just sing about a few and we'll probably hit it!" Dear friends, Jesus only had one mission. He left heaven and came to earth for one reason. "For the Son of Man came to seek and to save what was lost" (Luke 19:10).


### APPLICATIONS FOR TODAY!


It is not that Bible authority is unimportant. And it is not that we may believe and practice as we like. We are not teaching that obedience to God is inconsequential. The person who does not set his heart upon obeying the Word of God cannot be saved. But God's "emphasis" of what is really important covers the *humanity of the devout!* This term describes those of whom I spoke in an earlier chapter. Those *right* in heart, *genuine* in life, but *honestly mistaken* in some matters of doctrine (cf. Matt. 15:1-9).

The Lordship of Jesus is an essential. You cannot be saved without a genuine and permanent commitment to Christ. Genuine commitment to His will, His way and His Word is equally essential. This is the only area of your life of which God demands one hundred percent. These two things are "of first importance" (I Cor. 15:1-3), "the more important matters of the law" (Matt. 23:23), "the only thing that counts" (Gal. 5:6).

There's a difference between the *humanity of the devout* and *intentional rebellion!* We have good, valid arguments on the instrumental music question. The cases of "Nadab and Abihu" (Lev. 10:1,2) and "Noah and the Ark" (Gen. 6) unfortunately do not fit! Nadab and Abihu rejected God's law and intentionally offered a strange fire of their own choosing. It is not fair to accuse our instrumental brethren of doing this. They are trying as hard as we to be true to the Book. It is a "hermeneutical" problem, not one of rejection and rebellion. If Noah had built the ark of oak instead of gopher wood ("cypress" NIV) it would have been rebellion and substitution. And I wonder how many of us would deny that trim, shingles and handles were of other materials? Or do we think the ark was one hundred percent gopher wood?

## SO WHAT DO WE DO ABOUT LAW?

Law was given to follow. Rebellion, rejection and substitution cannot be tolerated. Let us love God's law. Let us obey His commands. Let's be dead serious about Bible authority.

But let's also understand that grace covers our imperfections. The humanity of the devout. Our inabilities of both understanding and performance!

Give me the liberty of literary license in the following illustration. I dreamed I died and stood before Peter at the gate. He searched his list for my name. "Oh yes, Marvin Phillips. Here's your name. You have five points!" "Five points? What does that mean?" Peter said, "Well you have to have one hundred points to get in!" "Wait a minute," I said. "I preached for the great Garnett church of Christ in Tulsa, Oklahoma." He said, "Oh that's right. We'll give you five more points." "Yes, but I've done mission work in Australia and preached all over the world!" He said, "We'll give you five more points for that!" I was sweating by now! I said, "Wait a minute. I helped direct the annual Tulsa International Soul Winning Workshop. We drew twelve thousand people people every year from all over the world. Thousands were helped and motivated to greater work for Jesus!" Peter said, "Very well, five points more. That's twenty points you have!" "Twenty points," I wailed. "Nobody could get into heaven but for the grace of God!" "That's right," Peter said, "but it's worth eighty points!" Praise the Lord!

## LET'S GET OUR AIM RIGHT!

Paul said it best: "The important thing is that Christ is preached" (Phil. 1:18); that "Christ will be exalted in my body whether by life or by death. For to me, to live is Christ and to die is gain" (vv. 20,21). I call upon every Christian to focus on Jesus. Strive for perfect obedience to His will. Aim for the bull's-eye on the target. And praise God for judging us by the clarity of our aim, not our bowling score of accuracy or performance. Let us, as Hebrews 12:2 says, *"Fix our eyes on Jesus!"*

# 18

## THAT PERUVIAN HOUSEWIFE!

She haunts me. That nameless housewife in Peru. Actually she's not even a real person. She was an illustration from the pen of Victor Knowles, editor for *One Body*. Victor was appealing for fellowship and unity on a much simpler basis than many of us demand. His statement was:

Anything a Peruvian housewife cannot understand cannot be essential to salvation!

It's just got to be true! God did not write His Bible so difficult that only a few scholars could understand. Victor shares a fear of mine that many preachers will stand before God only to hear Him say, "Why did you make it so hard?"!

### AN APPEAL TO THE FAMILY OF GOD!

Let's not make fellowship depend on anything except

"essential matters." My list of "six essentials" is discussed elsewhere in this book. If scholars have to tell us what to believe that would make our salvation dependent on the understanding of other men. This is surely not so!

I appeal to my non-instrumental brethren. Hold your convictions firmly. Nothing is so sacred as our personal beliefs that come from long, prayerful study of the Bible. But don't demand that every brother agree with you on every issue from marriage and divorce to instrumental music.

I appeal to brethren on the extreme right. You have a dedication to God and His Word. You follow the same hermeneutic as the rest of the non-instrumental folks. Please don't insist that we give up Bible classes on Sunday, communion sets, kitchens and gymnasiums in order to fellowship the rest of us. Fellowship just can't be that difficult!

I appeal to brethren in what is known today as the "Discipling Movement" (leadership in Boston). Your intentions have been sterling. You have awakened in all of us a need to preach commitment, soul winning and world evangelism. But you have taken things too far. You are outside the Scriptures in your demands. The Peruvian houswife could never make it in your fellowship. Your prerequisites for baptism are more than in any of the conversion stories in the book of Acts. You would not accept the Philippian jailor since he was contacted at midnight and baptized before dawn of the same day. You would have discipled Simon the sorcerer much longer before you baptized him. If he had gone through your "counting the cost" course, he might not have had the problems scripture says he had after baptism. But the fact remains, inspired men didn't do it that way. Nor did they re-baptize him as you no doubt would have! You have removed freedom from God's children. They cannot move, start churches, or lead lost people to Christ except in ways Boston has specifically instructed. I appeal to you to make room in your theology and your hearts to fellowship even the simple and retarded children of God! If the Father accepts us, why not the rest of the family?

## LET'S QUIT FRUSTRATING THE GRACE OF GOD!

Our legalism has gotten us into a number of problems that have isolated us from one another! She shall remain anonymous, but she was the wife of one of our most well-known debaters of my boyhood days. His extreme legalism led her to leave the church. She wrote a book entitled, *In the Great Hand of God I Stand!* While respecting her husband as a man who believed, preached and lived his convictions, she said she could no longer go along with that brand of theology.

She gave an illustration of her husband's beliefs to which she could no longer subscribe. Three boys reached the "age of accountability" on the same Wednesday night (erroneous idea to begin with). One was baptized that night. One had been baptized the Sunday before. The third waited until the next Sunday to be baptized. He died before Sunday! According to her husband, boy number one was the only one saved. Boy number two's baptism was invalid since he was baptized before he reached the age of accountability. Boy number three died lost because he postponed his baptism four days.

This kind of teaching showed up in our misunderstanding of "and if the righteous *scarcely* be saved" (I Pet. 4:18 KJV). Preachers would talk about "being saved by the skin of your teeth." It was portrayed that we must work as hard as we can and then only barely make it. My friends, the saved will verily fly into Heaven by the Grace of God. And not because they are so good but because God is so good.

Grace covers what we *can't* do, not what we *won't* do. Grace is seen in God giving what we need, not what we

141

deserve. And grace, properly understood is the greatest motivation in the world for obedience, dedication, commitment and service! Paul said, "The love of Christ leaves me no choice" (II Cor. 5:14 NEB).

### MARVELOUSLY SIMPLE; SIMPLY MARVELOUS!

The words *simple* and *easy* are not the same! God's plan of salvation is indeed simple. Zig Ziglar once made the statement, "It doesn't take much of a man to be a Christian; but it does take *all* of that man!" And it doesn't take a bunch of American scholars to set it all in place.

Let's suppose the Bible is dropped from an airplane onto an uncivilized island. Let's further suppose they are able to read, understand, and obey it. Wouldn't they be Christians? And wouldn't their fellowship properly be understood to be a New Testament Church? Isn't the Word of God the *seed* of the kingdom (Luke 8:11)? And doesn't seed reproduce after its kind? My, it's so simple! Now they would be all God wants them to be. But they would be uncontaminated by the issues and items that divide God's people in the civilized world. That Peruvian housewife would fit right in. So should we!

I put in a tour of duty in Korea with the United States Air Force. While there, I came in contact with a group of Korean Christians. I asked their preacher, "How did this church begin?" He held up his Bible. I said, "No, what American missionary came here and taught you these things?" He didn't seem to know what I was talking about.

He finally explained the group's beginning. The Presbyterians had been doing work among refugees. They handed out Bibles to the people. Many of them began attending the Presbyterian church. Some others believed the Bible but thought the Presbyterian church had a lot of things in it they couldn't find in the Bible. They finally decided to meet on their own. Just Christians, following the Word of God! It was my exciting privilege to preach for them one Sunday. Simple! The seed is the Word of God! Seed reproduces after its kind.

Now these Korean churches did a lot of things different than I was used to in Texas. They removed their shoes before entering the church building. Upon entering, each one bowed on his knees with head to the floor in reverence to God. Communion bread was yellow, about a half inch thick. Communion wine was yellow! Many American Christians (especially preachers) would have trouble fellowshipping them. The lady from Peru would have fit right in. Same Jesus, same Bible. Same worship, service and lifestyle.

## OTHER MISSION FIELD EXAMPLES!

Otis Gatewood entered Germany as soon as World War II was over. He was once asked, "Are you teaching the German Christians to speak English?" "No, we don't!" The lady replied, "What a pity. Never to hear the gospel of Christ in English!" I wonder if the lady thought Jesus was American, wore a three-piece suit and preached from the King James translation of the Bible.

My family was in Australia at a time when about a dozen other American missionaries were there. Most of them being from the "Bible belt," they really got after the Aussies for wearing shorts in the summertime and engaging in "mixed swimming." One Aussie was asked what he thought of "mixed bathing." He replied that he was against it. He didn't think the bath tubs were big enough for that! I have noticed that the closer Christians live to the coast the less their stand against mixed swimming. One Australian lady complimented our emphasis by saying, "I'm so glad you're more interested in souls than kneecaps!"

I clipped out a news report about Swaziland. The miniskirt had been banned as being a threat to the morals of the country. I was about to say, "Good for them. We should do the same in America!" I read on to discover many women in that part of the country went bare above the waist!

Customs and cultures are going to vary nation to nation! The beautiful thing is that the Word of God can be preached line for line in any country in the world. Many will receive it and commit their lives to it. But fellowship will be disrupted when we insist on our customs and our opinions on every subject.

## SIMPLICITY APPLIED!

I appeal for a "back to the Bible" movement! That sounds like it's right up our alley. And it is! Let's return to the simplicity of worship of the early Christians. Let Scripture guide our lifestyles. But let's not burden our brothers and sisters down with volumes of creeds, written or unwritten. The restoration slogan went, "Where the Bible is silent, we are silent!" We have amended it to read, "Where the Bible is silent we *hold strong opinions!*" Let's quit making these as tests of fellowship!

Christianity: simple as ABC!

A - Accepting the Sovereignty of God.

B - Believing and obeying the facts of the gospel.

C - Committing our lives to serving Jesus Christ.

Listen to this warning from the mighty apostle Paul:

> But I fear, lest by any means as the serpent beguiled Eve through his subtlety, so your minds should be corrupted from the *simplicity* that is in Christ! (II Cor. 11:3 KJV)

My hope (and yours) lies in this beautiful assurance from the Psalms:

The Lord protects the simplehearted; when I was in great need, he saved me! (Psa. 116:6)

Be careful when forming your theology on matters of faith and matters of opinion. Before you draw lines of fellowship remember that Peruvian housewife!

# 19

## MULES CAN'T KICK WHILE PULLING AND CAN'T PULL WHILE KICKING!

American Christians enjoy the luxury of criticizing and complaining. We've got comfortable buildings in which to meet. We have a well-paid staff to "do our Christianity" for us. Our preachers become our pitchers. And like baseball, when things aren't going our way we yell, "Throw the bum out!" We want a new pitcher (preacher)! That's part of the problem. We picture ourselves in the grandstand rather than on the playing field. So modern churches are filled with members demanding to be served. Threatening to leave if things don't go to please them.

A brotherhood is afflicted with the same disease. Each congregation, or each "branch" of the Restoration Movement has plenty. Plenty of buildings, preachers and members. We are like the church in Laodicea of whom it was said, "I am rich; I have acquired wealth and do not need a thing. But you do not realize that you are wretched, pitiful, poor, blind and

147

naked." (Rev. 3:17). In this spiritual stupor it is no wonder we take a "Who needs them?" attitude toward those with whom we differ.

## PULLING AND KICKING IN THE EARLY CHURCH!

I've noticed this pattern in the book of Acts. First there was great evangelism. "Three thousand souls were added," "daily additions," "the number of men grew to about five thousand," "more and more were added to their number" and "they rejoiced that they were counted worthy of suffering disgrace for the Name" (Acts 2:41,47; 4:4; 5:14,41). This was amidst persecution (leaders put in prison, Acts 4,5). But it was also a period of great unity and harmony in the church. "All the believers were one in heart and mind . . . and with great power" (Acts 4:32,33).

Then problems came. Criticism and jealousy over who was being fed and who was being neglected in their benevolence program. It is significant that this problem came after their numbers had swelled into the thousands and Christians were enjoying the favor of the community. Things got easy. When the pulling stops the kicking will start. It will ever be so!

Their solution to this problem is significant! They called the church together. They gave everyone input to the problem. The whole church appointed seven men to direct the feeding program. But the apostles "gave their attention to prayer and the ministry of the Word" (Acts 6:2,4). The kicking stopped. They kept everyone pulling!

## GREATEST PRINCIPLE ON CHURCH GROWTH!

I heard the story of the tower of Babel when just a lad in

Sunday School. Genesis chapter six. It was told about like this: "Some mean men wanted to build a tower taller than anyone had ever built. God didn't want them to build it. He changed their languages and scattered them all over the world. Boys and girls that's how we came to speak different languages and live in different parts of the world!" That's about all I knew about the tower of Babel for the next thirty years of my life.

Then one day, as a preacher trying to build a great church, I was reading that story again. It set me afire!

If as one people speaking the same language they have begun to do this, then nothing they plan to do will be impossible for them! (Gen. 11:6)

These people were not the people of God. The project they were attempting was not the will of God. Yet God said, "Nothing will be impossible for them!" I got to thinking, "We *are* the people of God. Our project is God ordained and blood bought. Jesus wants the world saved. His gospel is the saving message. His church is the agency of reconciliation. What if we apply the same four principles?"

1. The people are one: They work together!
2. They have one language: Singleness of purpose!
3. They plan (dream): They set big goals!
4. They "do" (work): They are people of action!

If we apply these principles and plug in the "God factor," our efforts will be blessed with success.

Now to him who is able to do immeasurably more than all we ask or imagine, according to his power that is at work within us! (Eph. 3:20)

This plan would stop the kicking. It would resume the pulling. Impossible things would become possible!

## IT IS IMPORTANT THAT EACH CHRISTIAN PULL!

Church growth occurs when every Christian stands together. As each one does his job faithfully, the church grows and becomes mighty (Eph. 4:16). We are all members of the body of Christ. Consider these thoughts from I Corinthians 12:12-26:

> The members are many but they form one body (v. 12).
> Feet, hands, eyes, ears are equally needed (vv. 15-17).
> God put each member in the body just as he wanted them to be (v. 18).
> Every part needs all the others (vv. 21-24).
> No division; equal concern for each other (v. 25).
> We should suffer and/or be honored together (v. 26).

Every part is different, needed, essential and valuable. My car broke down on the coldest day of the year. I was out making calls. It was snowing. The engine just quit. Do you know what was wrong? I needed a two dollar filter. And because that one little part wasn't doing its job an entire automobile was rendered useless.

It was only a three inch bolt. It probably felt insignificant. There were plenty of other parts. Let them do my job. So the little bolt did not function that day. And a giant DC-10 crashed because of it. Nearly three hundred people died in one of America's greatest air tragedies. We are all needed. To pull, not to kick! But we can't pull while we're kicking!

I repeat that we must stand for all the essentials! At all cost! But luxury, ease, apathy and laziness has descended upon us. The resultant kicking has brought us to suspicion, separation and sectarianism! We need to get back to pulling. Soul winning is our job. It is the only thing that counts!

## EACH MAN HELD HIS POSITION!

The beautiful story of Gideon is full of exciting lessons

(Jdgs. 7,8). The Midianites had really whipped up on the people of God. Israel was in pitiful defeat. It bothered God. It bothers God today! The Lord spoke to Gideon.

"You have too many men" (v. 2). God said, "I can't deliver you with that many. You'll say you did it by your own power." Churches today have tried all sorts of gimmicks to get "numbers." And as a result our ranks are full of the unconverted and uncommitted! Shall we put them out? God forbid! But don't *accept* nominal Christianity! God judges us as much by what we put up with as by what we practice. My family returned from seven years' mission in Australia. I got a call from Stanley Shipp. He said, "You've got a lot to get used to in America and I hope you never do!" I've never forgotten those words. We have too little leaning on God and too much relying on our own ingenuity. "Too little Spirit, too much human effort" (Gal. 3:3).

"Send the fearful home" (v. 3). God instructed Gideon to let all those who were afraid go home. And of thirty-two thousand men, twenty-two thousand left. I wonder if this is an accurate ratio today? More than eighty times Scripture says, "Do not be afraid!" Why are we yet so fearful? Fearful men can't pull! Fearful men will kick!

The test of watchfulness (v. 4)! The ten thousand were sent down to the river for a drink. God said, "Put them in two camps. Those that put their faces to the water on one side. Those who raise the water to their mouths and drink on the other side." The former could not see the enemy coming. The latter were the watchful ones. God said, "Take them." The army was now reduced to three hundred men. "With these three hundred men I will save you" (v. 7).

*FORMULA FOR VICTORY!*

1. The Providence of God! Four times in the story (vv.

151

7,9,14,15) God said, "I will save you; I will deliver them into your hands!" Victory is given the people who lean on God's power!

2. Good leadership! Gideon was God's man. A man in touch with God. "The Lord said to Gideon" (vv. 2,4,5,7,9). He had "put out the fleece" (6:36-40). Our leaders must be men totally given to God's leadership.

3. A good plan of action! To fail to plan is to plan to fail! Gideon divided his little band into three groups of one hundred each. He gave each a trumpet, an empty jar and a torch. Strange tools with which to go to war! And the odds were 120,000 to 300 (8:10).

4. "Each man held his position" (v. 21). Gideon said "Do exactly as I do." People will follow a leader who shows the way. Rulers give orders from the rear. Leaders are always out front showing the way. They went in the middle of the night. Gideon had them surround the Midianite camp. At his signal they all broke their pitchers, held up their torches, and shouted as one man, "A sword for the Lord and a sword for Gideon." Well, you know what it was. Just three hundred men decidedly unarmed. But you know what it *sounded* like! It sounded like three hundred *armies*! In the dark and confusion the Midianites turned on each other. There were one hundred and twenty thousand casualties.

The victory could never have been won with a bunch of "kickers." If anyone had not held his position, Midian would have spotted a hole in that circle and burst through it like a cannon! Nobody was kicking. They were all pulling. And the victory was won!

I was once told the difference between mules and zebras when they are attacked by wolves. Mules will react individually and disaster will follow. Zebras will group closely together. They form a circle, heads together, feet kicking in a solid, protective wall. They can fight off almost any enemy.

A lost world has only one hope: Jesus Christ, the gospel of

Christ and the church of Christ. Now we can kick each other to pieces. Or we can pull together and save ourselves and others. We can pull, or we can kick. But we can't do both! What about you?

# 20

## A MILLION PAIRS OF FROG LEGS!

Consider what a great forest is set on fire by a small spark! (James 3:5).

John had finally had it living in the city. He bought a house on acreage out in the country. He would escape the noise and trauma of city life. He would commute to work. But like most of us city boys he'd grown used to the sounds of the city. His first night in the country was not what he expected. He couldn't sleep. The "silence" was deafening. More than that, there was a small pond on the farm he had bought. The frogs began their croaking. It was like they were in the room with him.

But John was an entrepreneur! He remembered that people paid good money for frog legs. He knew a restaurant owner. He knew an opportunity when he saw one. The next day he contacted his friend. Could he use a million pairs? No, but he knew lots of other restaurant owners. Together they mapped their plans. John to supply. His friend to market. They made a fortune on paper right there.

It was John's job now to produce the frog legs. Can you imagine his consternation the next morning when he presented his restaurant owner friend with two scrawny pairs of frog legs? He meekly said, "Well, it sounded like a million!"

## EXAGGERATION IS A COMMON PROBLEM!

"I've told you a million times!" "I'm going to kill that kid!" Probably not! It's a simple case of exaggeration. We often give our problems a size they do not deserve. It is the same with criticisms and opposition. We often let it hinder our progress by overrating it!

My first ministry was in a little Texas town. Population eleven hundred. Church size about ninety members. And being the young, immature, brash preacher I was, I soon had some of the members stirred up. I wasn't used to criticism!

There was a little country store at the edge of town. You know the kind. You could buy groceries or fill your car with gas from the single pump. Lee Montgomery owned and operated it. He was my father confessor. "Lee," I said, "I'm quitting. The whole church is mad at me!" Lee replied, "The whole church is mad at you? Name them!" Well I said, "Tessie McGray is mad at me!" Lee said, "She sure is. Go on!" "Well, Mable Lacey is mad at me!" Lee agreed. "Go on!" "Well . . . ." I couldn't come up with a third name! And while I was scratching for the name of someone else who was mad, Lee said for effect, "The whole church is mad at you!" It taught me a valuable lesson.

## CRITICISM AND OPPOSITION ARE NOT NEW PROBLEMS!

Jealousy broke out between the herdsmen of Abraham and Lot. They disagreed about boundaries and whose cattle were whose. Thank God for an Abraham who said, "Let's not have any quarreling between you and me, or between your herdsmen and mine, for we are brothers" (Gen. 13:8). We could use a good dose of that attitude today.

The Jerusalem church got into it over jealousy, criticism and disagreement over the care of their widows (Acts 6:1-6). Paul wrote to the Corinthian church, "Chloe's household has written me that there are quarrels among you"(I Cor. 1:11). Peter and Paul got into it over social prejudices. Peter freely associated with Gentile Christians. Then some Jewish Christians arrived. He discretely "drew back and separated himself" from the Gentiles. Paul said Peter "was to be blamed" and trouble followed.

We have the quarrelers, complainers and critics among us today. And they demand too much. They insist we believe as they believe, draw lines of fellowship where they draw them, or else! And they make a lot of noise in the brotherhood!

## THEIR BARK IS WORSE THAN THEIR BITE!

We have largely overrated those among us who are negative, oppose any fellowship discussions, and brand those who participate as "liberals!" We need to whittle our problems down to size. There are grand moves being made today to talk to those with whom we disagree. Brethren long to fellowship with other members of the Family. Compromise is not the aim. Fellowship is! A growing number of Christians want to sort out the essentials from the non-essentials. This causes trauma for those who are not sure of their salvation. I have found the more secure you are in what you believe, the less fearful you are in talking with anyone.

Some brotherhood publications, church bulletins and pulpits have sounded their denunciation of these talks. Especially with our instrumental brethren. Interestingly enough, I tried a few years ago to get representatives of the various "non-instrumental" groups to hold a discussion. I wrote one hundred churches urging them to come to Tulsa for two day of talks. Only sixteen replied. And the hardest task I ever had was to get speakers to speak. Imagine that! They were loud in accusation through their pulpits and bulletins, but didn't want to come speak face-to-face with no strings attached.

Do these critics represent the majority of our brotherhood? I don't think so at all! I was finishing giving a lecture on "Progress Made in Fellowship!" at the Tulsa Soul Winning Workshop. A well known Bible Professor from one of our leading colleges said, "Phillips, I figure you and I are in the mainstream of where our brotherhood is going!" I thought maybe he was going to chew me up and spit me out! And the more I talk to men of real stature, I find them wanting to shed our narrow view that "we are right and all who disagree with us are wrong and lost!" Truth has nothing of which to be afraid.

The hardliners are small and getting smaller. But they are loud! It is that latter feature that makes us give them a size that is undeserved. They thrive on response and debate. We'd do well to read and heed the following verse:

Without wood a fire goes out; without gossip a quarrel dies down. (Prov. 26:20)

We are sometimes more afraid of each other than we are of God. Many preachers who would love to come to some of the Restoration Forums do not dare to come. They fear being labeled, branded, cancelled or fired! And it is a very real fear!

There are those who act as the Brotherhood Mafia. There have been some very real character assassinations.

## WHAT THE BIBLE SAYS ABOUT
## CRITICISM AND OPPOSITION!

Let's take a walk through the book of Proverbs.

Pride only breeds quarrels. (13:10)
A hot tempered man stirs up dissension but a patient man calms a quarrel. (15:18)
Starting a quarrel is like breaching a dam; so drop the matter before a dispute breaks out. (17:14)
He who loves a quarrel, loves sin! (17:19)
It is to a man's honor to avoid strife, but every fool is quick to quarrel. (20:3)

A walk through the New Testament reveals the following. Corinth was quarreling over preachers (I Cor. 1:11). Things haven't changed much have they? In his second epistle to Corinth Paul feared he would find among them "quarreling, jealousy, outbursts of anger, factions, slander, gossip, arrogance and disorder" (II Cor. 12:20). Timothy was urged to stay away from "myths, genealogies that promote controversies rather than God's work" (I Tim. 1:4). Elders were instructed not to be quarrelsome (I Tim. 3:3). Again Timothy was warned against the "unhealthy interest in controversies and arguments that result in envy, quarreling, malicious talk, evil suspicions, and constant friction" (I Tim. 6:4). We are warned that arguing about things of no value "only ruins those who believe" (II Tim. 2:14). "Stay away from foolish and stupid arguments. They produce quarrels and evidence that men have been caught in the Devil's trap" (II Tim. 2:23-26). Finally "avoid foolish arguments as being unprofitable and useless. Don't be divisive" (Titus 3:9).

I am aware that these verses might be used by one divisive person against another. Therefore I simply urge a deeper study of these verses and prayerfully ask God's help in absorbing them into our lives.

## MUCH UNITY ALREADY EXISTS!

While some preachers and publications do their best to keep the people of God separated, more and more Christians want to love the whole Family of God. This does not involve compromise of truth. No two brethren are alike on every issue. We may not all be right. We may not all be saved. But until God makes that distinction on Judgment Day we want fellowship with all the children of God.

It already exists on the mission field. It can get mighty lonely on the firing line where our missionaries have taken their families. They long for fellowship of other baptized believers. Many of them enjoy a marvelous friendship, fellowship and cooperation in ways they could not enjoy in America.

More and more churches are cooperating on joint projects. These include feeding the hungry. Bible school and soul winning materials. I have spoken on many joint fellowship "Spiritual Enrichment weekends" between Independent Christian Churches and non-instrumental churches of Christ. Brethren do so cautiously. And this is as it should be. But when we believe the same things, and our conscience and convictions are not violated, why not get together? Let those of us who preach unity so fervently be always ready to meet with, pray with and talk to those with whom we differ.

## THREE KEYS TO POWER!

For God did not give us a spirit of timidity, but a spirit of power, of love and of self-discipline! (II Tim. 1:7)

Churches have been held back by the fears and criticisms of men. I propose three keys which will keep us on the right track and growing despite opposition and criticism.

Key number one: *Be right!* I mean right with God and His Word. Do your study carefully. There is no substitute for having book, chapter and verse for all you believe and practice.

Key number two: *Be nice!* Speak the truth in love (Eph. 4:15)! "Let your conversation be always full of grace, seasoned with salt, so that you may know how to answer everyone" (Col. 4:6). We must be nice to all men especially to other members of God's same Family!

Key number three: *Be fearless!* More than eighty times the Bible says "Fear not!" "Don't be afraid!" And the keys, of necessity come in this order. Make sure you are right with the Bible. Make sure your attitude is Christ-like. Then "pedal-to-the-metal"! Don't let anything or anyone hold you back from doing the work God wants you to do. The frogs are still croaking. But it only sounds like a million.

# 21

## THE CROSS REDUCED TO KINDLING WOOD!

In this one body to reconcile both of them to God through the cross. (Eph. 2:16)

The cross! No piece of wood on the earth is so well known or so revered! We sing about the "Old Rugged Cross," "Jesus Keep Me Near the Cross," "When I Survey the Wondrous Cross"! Multiplied millions of crosses show up in all kinds of ways on Mother Earth. They adorn church buildings. They show up on religious greeting cards. They become jewelry for our fingers and our ears. They hang around our necks on chains.

And we love that old rugged cross! We love what it represents! We ask, "How much do you love us?" And Jesus' nail pierced hands outstretched on the cross answer, "This much!"

But the cross is a symbol of Christian unity. Jesus planned

through the cross to bring all the world together in Him! Read Eph. 2:14-18. The cross was meant to do several incredible things:

1. The cross spells out how bad sin is. It took the death of Jesus to redeem you for them!
2. The cross tells how valuable you are. Jesus thinks you're worth dying for!
3. The cross abolishes prejudice between Jew and Gentile.
4. The cross unites us with God.
5. And this is all done in the One Church which Jesus bought with His death on the cross (vs. 16, cf. Acts 20:28).

When the Bible was finished, and the sacred pen laid down, the people of God were one. They were members of the same church. No differing denominations existed. They had their differences. But they were able to worship together in love. There is no Bible example of one church branding another church. There is no instruction not to worship with a particular church because they were "liberal" or "anti." Corinth would have been a good excuse to do so. But it is glaringly absent.

What Jesus wanted was the unity of His people. He paid for it on the cross. Contrast Jesus' plan for unity with what we see in the religious world today.


## THE TENDENCY FOR PEOPLE TO DIVIDE!

The problem of fellowship is not just a religious problem. People seem bent on disagreeing, separating and fighting. Both Korea and Viet Nam have been divided into North and South because of different political ideologies. Thousands of people have died in those wars, including may Americans.

Revolutions currently sweep through Germany, Russia,

Rumania, Czechoslovakia and Poland. America was cut in half at the waist less than one hundred fifty years ago. Slavery was the issue. Families were divided. Brother shot brother. It was a dark time in American history.

Religious divisions have had their bloodshed too. Ireland is divided into Catholic and Protestant. They bomb each other "In the name of Jesus (?)"! Headlines scream "Christians bomb Lebanon"!

## APOSTASY, REFORMATION, RESTORATION!

The early church extended fellowship to the whole family of God! To be sure they had differences. And these caused problems. Some would eat meat offered to idols; some would not! Some stated bluntly "Gentiles cannot be saved unless they are circumcised and keep the law of Moses." Some doubted the resurrection. Some made the Lord's supper into a common disorderly meal. They tried to deal with these problems with the word of God. But without separation, division and starting other churches. Paul moved freely among the churches "preaching the same thing in every church" (I Cor. 4:17).

It took almost three hundred years for a hierarchy to develop in the church. An innocent practice of allowing one elder more power than another developed gradually to "area Bishops." Who could believe that within six hundred years a universal Pope would be appointed as "head of the church on earth"?

Martin Luther and others recognized the difference between the religion they saw and the original church of Christ. They called for "Reformation." The plea was good and needed! But in the next three hundred years the plea had crystallized into hundreds of warring denominations. All with different names, creeds and beliefs. Families couldn't even worship God together.

Great men began to appeal for a "Back to the Bible" movement. They could see that Jesus never intended Christians to be divided into different denominations. They rallied people around such slogans as:

The preaching of the Bible only makes Christians only!

Let us speak where the Bible speaks,
Let us be silent where the Bible is silent.
Call Bible things by Bible names.
Do Bible things in Bible ways!

In matters of faith, unity.
In matters of opinion, liberty.
In all things, charity!

It was a terrific plea. There has been none better on earth. It called for people to be "Christians only." The plea was often stated,

*We are Christians only; not the only Christians!*

It is interesting to note what happened to that plea that was so powerful and relevant at the turn of the nineteenth century.

## RESTORATION MOVEMENT SPLIT INTO THREE BRANCHES!

Isn't it interesting (and sad) that a plea to unite the people of God into one fellowship would, itself, be destined for division? There are, today, three main heirs to the Restoration Plea.

The Disciples of Christ churches. Signs in front of their buildings commonly use the term "First Christian Church" usually with "Disciples of Christ" added to distinguish them from other Christian churches. They have since taken a very liberal stance, abandoning for the most part, the Restoration Plea.

The Independent Christian churches have strong differences with their "Disciples" counterpart. Both use the sign, "Christian Church," but little similarity follows. Their doctrinal stance is the same as their non-instrumental brothers. They believe in the one church, baptism for remission of sins, weekly communion and have elders and deacons. Within their ranks are many instrumental churches of Christ. There are liberal and conservative churches among them.

The non-instrumental churches of Christ have the worst record of dividing among ourselves. Our hermeneutic which is the source of our strong Biblical stand is, unfortunately, also our achilles heel. I am ashamed to say there are few churches in the world more divided among themselves than we are. Many members of the churches of Christ do not know this. The following may be a shock to you.

*Where the Saints Meet* (alluded to in an earlier chapter) is a directory of non-instrumental churches of Christ. It is published by the Firm Foundation Publishing Co., and is edited by Mack Lynn, chairman of the Bible Department, David Lipscomb College in Nashville, Tennessee. It lists the following codes for identifying "different kinds" of churches of Christ:

AD70   Churches who believe Jesus' Second Coming was in 70 A.D.

CH   Charismatic

E   Less attention to traditional issues; more open to persons among denominations!

H   Believe women must wear head coverings in assemblies.

JO   Baptize in the name of Jesus only!

| | |
|---|---|
| ME | Mutual edification; opposed to "one preacher" system. |
| NB | Opposed to church ownership of buildings. |
| NBHS | Opposed to church ownership of buildings. Believes in Baptism of Holy Spirit for today! |
| NC | Non class. |
| NCp | Non class. But believes in located preacher. |
| MI | Non Institutional. |
| OC | One Cup. |
| OCA | One cup of unfermented grape juice; one loaf divided only as participants take own portion. |
| OCb | One cup of unfermented grape juice; loaf broken before distribution. |
| OCc | One cup of fermented grape juice. |
| OC + c | One cup; but with separate classes! |
| PM | Premillennial. |
| PMm | Premillennial; opposed to located preachers! |

Now this is in addition to the "Regulars" (main stream of churches of Christ). And it is sad to say there is "strained fellowship" between many of them. That's twenty divisions! *Each with the same hermeneutic!* Each demanding command, example or necessary inference as Bible authority. Now there's nothing wrong with the hermeneutic. What's wrong is our judgmentalism and sectarian spirit!

Someone has to call a halt to this. We have shattered the blood-stained cross of Calvary with our shameful divisions. The Texans rallied around the cry, "Remember the Alamo!" We must do the same thing. "Remember the Old Rugged Cross!" Let the cross pull us back across our precious convictions.

"Sameness" is out of the question. Must we all give up every practice opposed by the most conservative church in the list? Is this the way to have the unity for which Jesus died? Surely we realize "sameness" is unnecessary besides being impossible!

"Unity in diversity" is the only sane, sensible, scriptural

course of action. This scares many sincere Bible believers. They think it means compromise with truth. But it is not truth that is under attack. Truth has not caused our divisions. Insisting that everyone agree with us on every opinion is the culprit! The Restoration slogans are still valid:

In matters of faith, let's have unity!
In matters of opinion, let us have liberty!
In all things, let us have love!

When "The Book" says it, let's preach it! Let's do the best we can with matters of interpretation. "Where the Bible is silent, let's be silent!" Let's refuse to draw lines of fellowship on non-essential matters . . . for *we are brothers*!

# 22

## ALL HAIL THE POWER OF JESUS' NAME!

I consider it absolutely essential that you read the following lengthy text. And you might want to take off your shoes for the ground on which you will be standing is holy ground.

He is the image of the invisible God, the firstborn over all creation. For by him all things were created: things in heaven and on earth, visible and invisible, whether thrones or powers or rulers or authorities; all things were created by him and for him. He is before all things, and in him all things hold together. And he is the head of the body, the church; he is the beginning and the firstborn from among the dead, so that in everything he might have the supremacy. For God was pleased to have all his fullness dwell in him, and through him to reconcile to himself all things, whether things on earth or things in heaven, by making peace through his blood, shed on the cross.

Once you were alienated from God and were enemies in your minds because of your evil behavior. But now he has reconciled you by Christ's physical body through death to present you holy in his sight, without blemish and free from accusation — if you continue in your faith, established and firm, not moved from the hope held out in the gospel. This is the gospel that you heard and that has been proclaimed to every creature under heaven, and of which I, Paul, have become a servant.

Now I rejoice in what was suffered for you, and I fill up in my flesh what is still lacking in regard to Christ's afflictions, for the sake of his body, which is the church. I have become its servant by the commission God gave me to present to you the word of God in its fullness — the mystery that has been kept hidden for ages and generations, but is now disclosed to the saints. To them God has chosen to make known among the Gentiles the glorious riches of this mystery, which is *Christ in you, the hope of glory.* Col. 1:15-27

What a text! What a Jesus! The Image of the invisible God! All things created by and for Him! He holds all things together. He's the head of the church. He has supremacy in everything. God's fullness dwells in Him. Men are reconciled to God through Him. He's able to present us holy, spotless and without accusation to God! The glorious mystery of God is *Christ in you, the hope of glory!*

We'll never be able to unite the people of God on anything less than Jesus! Our issues won't do it! Our best efforts at hermeneutics won't bring it. The only way to unite us short of Jesus is on the convictions of the most conservative church among us. The rest of us will have to give up all they feel is unscriptural and unauthorized. We'll have to give up Bible classes, communion cups, preachers, church buildings and a ton of other things.

Even this won't do it. For some of these conclusions contradict each other. How partake the Lord's supper with both fermented and unfermented grape juice? How partake on "Saturday only" and "Sunday only"? Clearly the unity for which Jesus prayed and died is found elsewhere! We need to look for it!

## OUR PURPOSE IS OBSCURE IN THE WORLD TODAY!

The world doesn't know what the Restoration Movement is all about. They mostly do not know that either Christian churches or churches of Christ exist. Those who do know about us consider us weak, ineffective and full of scandal.

To the denominational world our purpose is obscure. Ask them, "What do you know about the churches of Christ?" You'll usually get two answers. "They're the ones who don't use instrumental music." Or, "They think they're the only ones going to heaven!"

Our purpose is obscure to many within restoration churches themselves. Many can't define the "Restoration Movement." They do not know what it is all about. Many do not know about the three main divisions. Most could not name the "splinter groups" that have sprung up all over the country. Between many sister congregations there is isolation, suspicion and jealousy!

The purpose of the church is obscure to many members of a local congregation. We devote our time to routine church services, meeting the budget and involvement in some ministry. We deal mainly with superficial things. We have forgotten that the "Son of Man came to seek and to save what was lost" (Luke 19:10).

## REDISCOVERING THE CENTER OF
## POWER AND IDENTITY!

What would you say is the most often read scripture in church services today? Acts 2:38? Romans 16:16? Would it be verses on God's plan of salvation? If anything I believe it would be those scriptures read as Christians participate in communion! It will be from I Cor. 11:23-30 or one of the gospel accounts when Jesus instituted the Lord's supper. The bread is the body of *Christ*; the cup, the blood of *Christ*. We partake in remembrance of *Christ*; to show forth *Christ's* death until He comes.

And we sing about Christ and the cross to "prepare our minds for the observance of the Lord's supper"! We sing "The Old Rugged Cross," "Jesus Keep Me Near the Cross," "When I Survey the Wondrous Cross."

When one comes for baptism we do not ask him, "What translation of the New Testament do you read?" We don't ask him what gospel paper he takes. We don't even ask him how he believes about instrumental music, orphan homes or church cooperation. We ask, "Do you believe *Jesus Christ is the Son of God?*"

Jesus is the powerful, unifying center of who we are and what we represent! That question asked before baptism identifies that Jesus is accepted as the Son of God; the Lord of our lives. He alone is the Giver of salvation.

I am the way and the truth and the life. No one comes to the Father except through me. (John 14:6)

Salvation is found in no one else, for there is no other name under heaven given to men by which we must be saved. (Acts 4:12)

We'll finally stand before Jesus' throne alone (II Cor. 5:10).

## WE CAN UNITE IN JESUS' NAME!

All hail the power of Jesus' name.
Let angels prostrate fall.
Bring forth the royal diadem,
And crown Him Lord of all!

Jesus is our force for "drawing together"! He is the center

piece of our religious feast. As one grand old song says, "*Jesus*, there's just something about that name!" Vertical unity with Him brings horizontal unity with each other. I urge you to rethink who Jesus really is. Do you feel about the cross like Jesus felt? Do you feel about His "church family" like He does? Don't try to draw near to God and distance yourself from His childern! Fathers love their kids. All their kids!

Restudy the commitment you've made to Jesus Christ! Have you been baptized into Christ? Have you given Him complete control as Lord of your life? There was a little chorus the children sang in Australia:

If you don't crown Him Lord *of all,*
Then you can't crown Him Lord *at all!*

Do you belong to His church? Are you living daily for Him? Are you sharing His good news with all you meet? It is in our commitment to Jesus Christ that we have hope of reunion on earth before reunion in heaven.

# 23

## CONVICTION AND COMPASSION
## AT CORINTH!

I have many people in this city. (Acts 18:10)

There were a thousand prostitutes in Corinth. All from the temple of Aphrodite, goddess of love. Their pagan temple sat on the highest mountain in easy view of the thousands thronging Corinth's busy streets. And there were lots of sailors. Corinth was a regular port of call for ships on their way to Rome. Sailors who had been at sea a long time. Lots of money in their pockets. Lots of time on their hands. They were easy trade for those loose women whose hair was shamelessly cropped and who wore no traditional veils over their faces. They wanted to be seen, quickly recognized so they could get on with their business. Guides say their sandals were fixed so they could leave imprints in the sand which said, "follow me"! Corinth was high in venereal disease. Every kind of wickedness was common there. That was its reputation. When you wanted to insult a man you called him a "Corinthian"!

If we had sent a mission survey team to Corinth, their report likely would have been, "We can't build a good church here!" Paul surveyed the same city and said, "We *must* start a church here!"

## BEGINNING OF THE CHURCH IN CORINTH!

The story is told in Acts chapter eighteen. Paul, along with Silas and Timothy, came there on his second missionary trip. Paul got a job as a tent maker with Aquila and Priscilla and preached Christ in the synagogue every Saturday. Many heard, believed and became Christians. Others were abusive and caused trouble (vs. 6). God reassured Paul with the words, "I have much people in this city" (Acts 18:10). So he stayed in Corinth for eighteen months continuing to preach and teach about Jesus!

Two verses tell of the great success of Paul's stay in that wicked city.

> Many of the Corinthians who heard him believed and were baptized. (Acts 18:8)
> Do you not know that the wicked will not inherit the kingdom of God? Do not be deceived: Neither the sexually immoral nor idolaters nor adulterers nor male prostitutes nor homosexual offenders, nor thieves nor the greedy nor drunkards nor slanderers nor swindlers will inherit the kingdom of God. *And that is what some of you were. But you were washed, you were sanctified, you were justified in the name of the Lord Jesus Christ and by the Spirit of our God!* (I Cor. 6:9-11)

I imagine Paul writing this with a smile on his face. Just look at the depths of sin these new Christians were rescued from. The song leader an ex-homosexual! The brother who led the opening prayer a converted male prostitute. And those who served communion that Sunday morning. One used to be a noted thief, that one an idol worshipper and that one a known drunk! Paul was so happy the gospel of Christ had won these precious sinners to Jesus. I'm not too sure they would fit in some of our fashionable churches today.

When you preach Christ in an environment like that you can expect two things. One, God's marvelous saving power will do its work. Two, when you convert folks from that atmosphere you will have lots of problems in their continuing service to Jesus. A church must be prepared to deal with that in a kind and compassionate manner! A large sign in a church foyer cautioned, *"Warning: Human beings worship here!"*

## THE CORINTHIAN CHURCH HAD
## EVERY KNOWN PROBLEM!

First and Second Corinthians are the two letters Paul wrote this church a few years later. They reveal what you might expect. Although these Christians were serious about their commitment to Christ, they had lots of problems. Nearly every chapter reveals a new problem.

There was the problem of sectarianism. The division was over preachers (I Cor. 1:11,12). The situation hasn't changed much has it!? One said, "I follow Paul"; others said, "I follow Apollos," or "Cephas." And perhaps in an arrogant way, others said, "I follow Christ"!

They had a moral problem so bad "it does not even occur among the pagans." "A man has his father's wife" (I Cor. 5:1). We don't know whether the man was having sexual relations with his own mother or stepmother. Either way it was a terrible problem for the Corinthian church.

And there were lawsuits among Christians too (I Cor. 6:1-8). Their court was held in the middle of the city. People could do their shopping and catch what was going on in court that day. It was the same Bema where Paul stood accused by the Jews. Where Gallio "showed no concern whatever" (Acts 18:17). I've seen it. It still stands among the ruins of the city. The public could see when Christians didn't get along and took each other to court. It was a sad example to set by folks trying to lead others to Christ.

Then came a whole list of problems in marriage. Paul discusses their questions at length in chapter seven. Then they had problems about eating meats which had been offered to idols (chapter eight). Some opposed support of preachers and that is discussed in chapter nine. Other chapters in First Corinthians deal with problems over the length of women's hair, their head coverings, their abuse of spiritual gifts, and even that some Christians were not yet convinced about resurrection.

Could you have worshipped at such a church then? Should that church have been branded and avoided by "faithful brethren"? It is interesting to see how the inspired apostle dealt with this.

## CONVICTIONS AT CORINTH!

Convictions were important at Corinth. And they are today! Paul never advocated compromise with the truth. The truth was preached when the church at Corinth was established. Paul "reasoned, persuaded and converted both Jews and Greeks." He stood on his convictions in spite of the danger to his life. He testified before the Roman Governor Gallio that "Jesus was the Christ" (Acts 18:5,12) at the very court where brother would later sue brother!

Paul preached against division in the Corinthian church (I Cor. 1:10). Chapter five is a scathing denunciation of immorality in the church and calls for withdrawal of fellowship from the unrepentant brother. Christians were sternly told not to take each other to court. "It is better to be cheated than to bring the church to shame before unbelievers" (I Cor. 6:7,8). Some of that preaching needs to make the rounds of the pulpits of today. The abuses of spiritual gifts were soundly dealt with in chapter fourteen. And a clear stand was taken in chapter fifteen on the resurrection; Christ's and ours!

What I'm saying is that in this precious church they had lots of problems. The plain, pure Word of God was preached on every subject. There was no effort to wink at sin or to compromise truth. But how was fellowship with this church and within this church viewed?

## TRUTH PREACHED; COMPASSION SHOWN!

The church at Corinth may not be recognized by many as a true church of Christ today. To be sure, they had lots of problems. Their preacher might be marked, criticized and written up in brotherhood papers. How were they treated by other contemporary Christians?

Paul recognized they were truly a "church of God" (I Cor. 1:2). He wrote "I always thank God for you" (1:4). He said, they were "enriched in every way," "had all the spiritual gifts," and was confident God would keep them strong to the end and stand them blameless before God" (1:5-8).

Chapter sixteen shows his love and tolerance for this church in its struggles to be a New Testament church. He was going to visit them again and stay with them for awhile (vv. 5,6). Timothy was coming to preach and work among them (v. 10). Apollos was being sent to preach for them (v. 12). Paul thanked them for their financial support which he received from the hands of Stephanas, Fortunatas, and Achaicus (vv. 17,18). Other churches in the province of Asia sent greetings with warm affection (vv. 19,20). Paul closed his epistle to

181

them with the words, "My love to all of you in Christ Jesus. Amen" (v. 24).

## SUMMARY

Corinth is an example of Christian fellowship to us today. It took the gospel of Christ to save them. When their conduct was wrong they were chastised with the Word of God. When they were doctrinally wrong Paul wrote in loving correction. Truth was never compromised. But fellowship was withheld *only* to the brother who would not repent of his gross immorality. Mention is freely given of Paul's love for this church. Faithful preachers freely went there to preach, teach and enjoy the fellowship. The churches of the area extended fellowship, love and greeting.

If the church at Corinth can be considered worthy of fellowship, there is hope for us all! Let's be motivated by this Biblical example. Let us learn the delicate, but very real balance of our convictions, our compassion and our fellowship!

## 24

# WE NEED ALL THE FELLOWSHIP
# WE CAN GET!

It is right for me to feel this way about all of you, since I have you in my heart; for whether I am in chains or defending and confirming the gospel, all of you share in God's grace with me. God can testify how I long for all of you with the affection of Christ Jesus. (Phil. 1:7,9)

One of the greatest things about the early church was their sweet fellowship. The above text says it marvelously. "It is right to feel this way about you!" "You're deep in my heart." "I long for you!" "The affection we share is that of Jesus Christ!"

This love God's people have felt for one another has been shared from generation to generation. It is exemplified when today's church gathers for worship and praise. I love watching the smiles, hearing the "Amens" and holding the hands of my brothers and sisters as we sing, "We're part of a family that's been born again . . . ." Song writers have picked up on this beautiful relationship God's people enjoy. "What a Fellowship!" The singing group Acappella has an album out called "Sweet Fellowship!" It is a marvelous song. It is a marvelous blessing.

### FELLOWSHIP IN THE EARLY CHURCH!

The very first Christians "devoted themselves to . . . fellowship" (Acts 2:42). Fellowship is defined as "having a part in or a relationship with" persons or things. There are at least three levels of fellowship mentioned in the Bible. We are called into *the fellowship* (I Cor. 1:9). Every scripturally baptized person on earth is in that fellowship. And vertical unity with God brings horizontal fellowship with all His children. Secondly there is fellowship between brothers and sisters in the family. "Fellowship with one another" (I John 1:7). Thirdly, there is fellowship with "things." "Have no fellowship with the unfruitful works of darkness" (Eph. 5:11, KJV). Baptism puts you into "The Fellowship." And we fellowship people and things that do not violate our convictions.

Peter urges, "Love the brotherhood of believers" (I Pet. 2:17). Love being with them. Love working with them. Love praising God with them. And the fellowship of God's people is so sweet.

But that fellowship is too scarce. There are so many who want to limit it. Too many want to play God. They want to be the Father. We're just the kids. Let's be true to the Father; true to His Word. But let's love our brothers and sisters just as God loves them. We need all the fellowship we can get!

### FELLOWSHIP WITHOUT COMPROMISE!

There are those who fear fellowship with those with

184

whom they disagree. Those they feel are in error. And to be sure, truth is never to be compromised. "Preach the Word" (II Tim. 4:2). Never compromise one line of scripture with anyone or anything on earth.

But all fellowship is not endorsement! We do not want to "bid God speed" to error!

> Anyone who runs ahead and does not continue in the teaching of Christ docs not have God; whoever continues in the teaching has both the Father and the Son. If anyone comes to you and does not bring this teaching, do not take him into your house or welcome him. Anyone who welcomes him shares in his wicked work. (II John vv. 9-11)

Does this verse teach you not to receive anyone in your house if he disagrees with you on any subject? Obviously not! There is a vast differrence in leaving the "teaching of Christ," and being mistaken about certain non-essential things. This verse obviously does not refer to Christ-preaching, Bible-believing Christians who may be wrong on some point of doctrine.

Truth is never to be sacrificed or compromised for anyone. I do not have to say the words "In Jesus' name" when I pray. But if I am intentionally asked to omit my Lord's name, count me out! I won't compromise what I believe about Jesus with anyone!

Please hold my feet to the fire on what I preach! Demand scripture for whatever I preach. But please don't tell me how to treat my brothers and sisters in Christ. God told me to love them and I'm going to do it. I am sometimes criticized because I preach in places other than "mainline Churches of Christ." There are no strings on my preaching. I will preach what I believe. But please judge me by *what* I say, not *where* I say it!

## LET'S FELLOWSHIP IN THINGS UPON WHICH WE AGREE!

Many churches use James Dobson's films on "The Family." Some have used Larry Burkett who gives an excellent seminar in money management. Many read and benefit from books and tapes by such men as Gene Getz and Chuck Swindoll.

But we especially need more fellowship between brethren in the "same church"! More and more "cross-fellowship" discussions are cropping up around the country. I remember one to which I was invited a few years back in Portland, Oregon. It was sponsored by the Crossroads Church of Christ (Instrumental). Don DeWelt and Victor Knowles represented the instrumentals. Gary Elliott (President of Columbia Christian College) and I represented the non-instrumental side. Gary had never participated in one of these things before. He asked me what to expect. I said, "They'll ask you some very specific questions and they'll want clear, specific answers. But they'll love you and you'll enjoy it!" I was right on all counts. What a wonderful opportunity for brethren who love truth and each other to get together.

More and more churches plan "joint fellowship" ventures. Many of my speaking engagements are "Spiritual Enrichment Weekends" jointly attended by both instrumental and non-instrumental brethren. I recently did a "Family Life Week" seminar with an instrumental church. Acappella brethren came too. The fellowship was rich indeed. We have much more in common than not!

## WHAT ABOUT "COME OUT FROM AMONG THEM"?

"Therefore come out from among them and be separate. Touch no unclean thing, and I will receive you" (II Cor. 6:17). It is important to read the whole paragraph (vv. 14-18).

God doesn't want us "yoked together with unbelievers." He says Christians are to have no fellowship with "unbelievers, wickedness, darkness, Belial or idolatry." Then follows, "Come out from among them"!

Are all "mistaken brethren" unbelievers, wicked people, darkness and idolators? If it takes doctrinal perfection to be a believer, how many would there be? But it does take faithfulness to God and genuine dedication to His will, way and Word!

Does "come out from them" mean separate from every brother with whom you disagree? Then with how many brethren could you fellowship? There aren't any two Christians on earth who agree on every point of doctrine.

We have elsewhere discussed six essentials. I separate from those who reject any of them. I do not find where God has instructed us to come out from anyone else! Find a scriptural example where God's people were instructed to separate from anyone holding to these six essential matters of faith! I do not know of any!


### FELLOWSHIP WITH GOD AND EACH OTHER!

The Bible talks about fellowship with God and each other in 1 John 6-9. I want to give you a paraphrase of them:

v. 6 God: "Don't play games with me. You don't need them. They won't work!"

v. 7 God: "Just 'walk in the light.' That way you'll have fellowship with Me and each other!"

Marvin: "God, I do want fellowship with you; and with my brethren. But that 'walking in the light.' I don't think I can live a 'perfect' life!"

v. 8 God: "I know you've got sins! Walking in the light doesn't mean 'sinless perfection.' I know you can't give me that. But you can be 'genuine'!"

187

Marvin: "One more thing, God. What do I do about my
     sins?"
v. 9 God: "Just confess them to me. Everytime you genuinely
     repent and confess your sins to me, I'll forgive
     them all!"
Marvin: "Wow!"

I'm not much on bumper stickers. Some people have
several on each bumper and on the back windshield. I saw
one the other day that read "Help Stamp Out Bumper
Stickers." Another read, "This is NOT a Bumper Sticker!" But
this one caught my eye. It said simply,

"Be Patient With Me;
God Isn't Finished With Me Yet!"

I'll get a lot of praise for writing this book. I will also take a lot
of flack! I like the former. But I also need the latter. My only
plea to my brethren is to give me the benefit of doubt. I'm
trying to be faithful to God. I want to be true to His Book. We
are fellow strugglers on this earth. The smartest of us makes
so many mistakes. The "most correct" among us is wrong so
many times and in so many ways. So let's be patient with each
other's struggles. We need all the fellowship we can get!

# 25

## THE WALLS MUST COME DOWN!

For he himself is our peace, who has made the two one and has destroyed the barrier, the dividing wall of hostility, by abolishing in his flesh the law with its commandments and regulations. His purpose was to create in himself one new man out of two, thus making peace, and in this one body to reconcile both of them to God through the cross, by which he put to death their hostility. He came and preached peace to you who were far away and peace to those who were near. For through him we both have access to the father by one Spirit.

Consequently, you are no longer foreigners and aliens, but fellow citizens with God's people and members of God's household, built on the foundation of the apostles and prophets, with Christ Jesus himself as the chief cornerstone. In him the whole building is joined together and rises to become a holy temple in the Lord. And in him you too are being built together to become a dwelling in which God lives by his Spirit. (Eph. 2:14-22)

Nov. 9, 1989. The wall is gone! Millions from East and

West Germany can be together again. World news monitored the joyous reunion. They cried, "We are all Germans!" "We are one people!" They sang, "Such a beautiful day should last forever!" No government or ideology will ever keep them apart again. I wish I'd been in Berlin the following Sunday. Television cameras failed to catch what no doubt happened. Christians once separated by a wall of shame were able to praise God together after so man years. There are so many lessons!

## BERLIN WALL: 1961-1989

The wall was built by the communists on Aug. 13, 1961. It was built to keep East Germans from fleeing to freedom in the West. Many were shot and killed trying to escape to freedom. On Nov. 9, 1989 it came down after twenty-eight years, two months, twenty-seven days.

I watched, my face glued to the television screen, as thousands poured over the border. Some were shouting and singing. Others came over in silence, shedding tears for the memories of being held apart from freedom and their loved ones. Strangers hugged one another in the streets. Relatives can now visit one another again.

The West German government gave each visitor showing an East German passport the equivalent of US$50.00. An estimated three million people have crossed the border. The West German government has given away twenty-five million dollars.

All the magazines covered the story. Time, Newsweek, US News and World Report. They showed pictures of people standing on the wall dancing, singing and celebrating. People chipped away at the wall with pick axes, hammers and whatever else they had. Some letting out their anger and frustration for that barrier. Others just wanted souvenirs.

What will happen next? It is anybody's guess! Will there be reunification? Someone suggested an East Germany "not alien to the West but different from it"! But one thing is sure. The wall is gone! No one can ever build it back. Once the people have tasted fellowship, no one will ever separate them again!

### JESUS CAME TO TEAR DOWN THE WALLS!

Back to that marvelous text (Eph. 2:14-22). The two greatest walls that have ever existed are addressed. The wall of sin beween men and God. And the wall between Jew and Gentile. No greater social segregation ever existed. Jews called Gentiles "dogs." God's exact purpose by sending His Son to the cross was to bring "togetherness;" brother to brother, man to God!

Jesus is our peace! He made Jew and Gentile "One"! He destroyed the barrier between them. He ended the wall of hostility. I'm using His exact words from the text. He made one new man out of the two. Both were reconciled to each other and to God by the cross of Jesus Christ. They ended up in one church; one family, the Family of God!

### WALLS THAT NEED TO COME DOWN TODAY!

The wall of social prejudice still stands today. Jesus died on the cross to destroy the wall between Jew and Gentile. New Testament epistles deal with the problems of bringing both together in the same church. But they were together. That was God's way. It is still God's way!

Poor Christians become children of the King in the church. Rich Christians become slaves to God and each other. James says both were to rejoice in this (James 1:9,10). In Christ Jesus we are *"neither Jew nor Greek, slave nor free, male nor female, for you are all one in Christ Jesus"* (Gal. 3:28). There is no room in the church for racial prejudice.

I wish I could say that in today's church there is no wall of racial prejudice. But after the cross of Christ, and after a civil war one hundred twenty-five years ago, we still have racially prejudiced churches. I don't believe in "black" churches. I don't believe in "white" churches. Let's just get together and be the Family of God. Heaven is a mixed neighborhood. God is a multi-colored God! Let the walls come down. Let the people of God rejoice and dance in the streets.

Then there are the walls of denominationalism. The Restoration plea is still needed and valid today. God didn't need more than one church anymore than He needed more than one Son! We urge upon our religious world today a "Back to the Bible" movement. People are tired of being told what to believe by councils and conventions; by religious hierarchies. Let there be an end to denominational creeds, laws, rules and divisions. Let's just be Christians. Let God be God! Let the Bible be recognized as our lone revelation of His will. Let us again,

> Speak where the Bible speaks,
> Remain silent where the Bible is silent.
> Call Bible things by Bible names,
> And do Bible things in Bible ways!

Let the walls between Restoration churches fall! They serve no purpose. They expose us to shame before an unbelieving world! The Restoration Forums are a fresh start. Brethren have begun to get together for study, prayer and discussion. Instrumental brethren are talking to their brothers of non-instrumental persuasion. Let no one be afraid. We've been added to the same church by the same Lord, and in the same way! We are together on the things that count. Let's hold fast to our convictions, but talk openly with sincere brethren with whom we disagree. Truth will stand the light of discussion and investigation.

And let these talks be multiplied all over the world. No one has a copyright on discussion. I'm happy to see local churches getting together to discuss their differences and celebrate their similarities. Let us talk to each other. Let us talk with each other. Let us visit one another. Joint ventures of study and prayer would be good. We really need to get to know one another. That which unites us is far greater than that which divides us.

Let the walls come down between non-instrumental churches of Christ. "Main stream" churches have their walls of separation. These walls aren't even coded in our directory of churches. But the walls exist none the less. Churches with petty jealousies. Two of the biggest problems we preachers face are with vanity and jealousy.

One Tulsa preacher said to me, "Our differences are too basic"! I suggested we get together to talk about it. We spent an hour and a half together. Not one time did he ever say, "the Bible says *this*, but you do *that!*" Most of our walls are not over doctrinal matters at all, but over fears and preferences! Brethren, please, don't divide over such petty things. A lost world needs us. Let the walls come down. From Tulsa to Tacoma. From Dallas to Detroit. From San Antonio to San Francisco. Let the walls come down. God has one Family. We are in it together! Let's begin to act like it!

Let's lose our fear of the brotherhood mafia. To be sure they are out there. Brotherhood wide publications will write you up, lie about you and warn others about you! Be sure you are right with God and His Word. Then fear no man! I plead with these publications. Stop being a spreader of rumors, suspicion and separation. Let's destroy walls not each other. Use your great power of influence to build up the body and save the lost from hell.

Let's make the Restoration Plea a "uniting" plea, not a "dividing" plea! We offer the world the best solution for unity as the people of God. Let's not repudiate the plea by our own divisive actions.

## THE CROSS IS A WALL DESTROYER!

The purpose of Christ's visit to earth was to destroy walls of separation. Sin is the greatest wall of all. *"Your iniquities have separated you from God"* (Isa. 59:2). Sin is the world's great problem. It is the epidemic that touches the lives of every acceptable person. And the wages of sin is death (Rom. 6:23). Spiritual separation from God. Jesus came, gave us the gospel and bought the church so we could be saved from our sins. The wall came down in Jerusalem in the year 33 A.D. with the words of Peter, *"repent and be baptized every one of you, in the name of Jesus Christ so that your sins may be forgiven"* (Acts 2:38). There was such rejoicing. Three thousand crossed the wall that day. They were baptized into Christ and were given forgiveness, the indwelling of the Holy Spirit and Jesus added them as saved people to His church (Acts 2:41,47).

Reunion is always on the mind of God. The story of the prodigal son (Luke 15:11-24) so graphically illustrates this truth. The boy ran away from home. He got into trouble. He finally woke up. Broke, alone and a failure! He made his decision to come home to the father. The father saw him coming when he was a long way off. He ran to his son! He kissed and embraced him. He welcomed him home with the biggest feast the boy could ever imagine. The boy did not deserve his father's goodness. And we don't either. But that's what we get. Not because we are so good, but because He is so good. Let's try to be as good to each other as God is to us!

194

## ARE THERE WALLS IN YOUR LIFE?

This book is basically about fellowship between brethren and churches who disagree. I urge you to get to know these good people. They love God as much as you do. They respect and believe in Bible authority as much as anyone could. Break down the wall. Discuss your differences. Respect others when you can't fellowship with them. But get all the fellowship you can!

What about other walls? Walls of separation between friends? Maybe in your marriage? Walls will stand as long as we let them. Someone needs to overcome pride and take the first step.

And last of all there is that wall of sin. We have a gospel that is powerful and a Jesus Who is willing. Don't stay lonely on the wrong side of the wall when you could be singing, dancing and enjoying the party. All things are ready. Come to the feast!

# 26

## I HAVE A DREAM!

Let the prophet who has a dream tell of his dream, but let the one who has my word speak it faithfully. (Jer. 23:28)

Two small brothers, Carl and Roy were sent to the little country store where their family traded. "Buy a can of coal oil," their mother said. She put a shiny dime in Roy's hand for the kerosene and a penny each for a treat.

There were some layabouts in front of the store who delighted in causing trouble for little boys. "You boys aren't brothers!" "Yes we are!" "No, you're not. You've got blue eyes. His eyes are brown! You're not brothers at all. Carl, the police brung you! They just found you and gave you to Roy's family to raise." It was all a lie. But it was just enough to cause doubt in Carl's mind.

The boys had always been inseparable. They had gotten along beautifully. Now Carl wasn't certain he was really a member of Roy's family. It was enough to cause a strain in the relationship. Where they had always gotten along, now they began to fight and argue constantly.

Carl's father took him aside. "Carl, you and Roy have always gotten along well. Now you're always fighting and arguing about something. What's wrong?" And Carl blurted it out. "I don't belong here. I ain't really a part of this family. The police brung me."

A wise father put his arm around Carl's shoulder. "Twelve years ago I took your mother to the hospital in town. The doctor laid Roy in my arms and said, 'You have a fine new baby boy.' Two years later we went back to that same hospital. Your mother gave birth to you. That same doctor brought you to me and said, 'You've got another fine boy!' You and Roy are brothers all right!"

That night Carl and Roy went to their room. They lay down on small beds across the room from each other. Carl didn't know how to say it. But in the dark he blurted out, "I ain't gonna fight you no more!"

I believe the reason brothers fight so much is because they are not really sure of their own standing with God. I've noticed the more I'm sure of what I believe; of who and whose I am, the less I want to fight with my brothers and sisters. I dream of a day that will be true for all the children in God's family.

## A DREAM OF "TOGETHERNESS"!

Do you remember that famous sermon by Martin Luther King, "I have a dream!"? His dream was for black and white to dwell side by side in equality. He dreamed for walls of hostility to come down and we would recognize the Fatherhood of God and the brotherhood of men. I have a similar dream for the people of God to one day be together!

To be sure there are obstacles to that dream. There are those who don't want it to happen and will oppose it. There are brethren who don't understand it and are afraid of it. Others wish it would happen. They are waiting for others to act first and then they'll join in. It will take leaders who have enough loyalty to God and love for His Word to stick their necks out and act on their dream.

## FACTS WE MUST ACCEPT!

Fact one: We *are* brothers! All those scripturally born again are in God's Family. We've been added to the same church! You and I have no say about that. Whether instrumental or non-instrumental, premillennial, cups or no cups, classes or non-class, we are brothers by virtue of the new birth. Jesus said "He that believeth and is baptized shall be saved" (Mark 16:16). We all did that and now claim that salvation promised by the Lord.

Fact two: The problem of instrumental music will never be solved on this earth. It is like other problems over which we differ. Divorce and remarriage is the subject of an annual seminar in Texas. The best arguments have been presented by both sides. The disagreement is serious. But little solution comes from those meetings. If we fellowship at all, it must be on what unites us, not what divides us!

Fact three: Fellowship with brethren with whom you disagree does not demand a compromise of truth or your convictions. Non-instrumental churches will still sing acappella. They will still hold strong convictions that it violates the hermeneutic they use in understanding the Bible. Fellowship between the churches must therefore be acappella. But respect is going to have to be given these brethren in their convictions.

Fact four: Divisiveness is worse than difference! It is not

possible that we all come to the same conclusions on all issues. But divisiveness is a choice! When we draw lines of fellowship on matters of "personal understanding" we stab another spear into the spiritual body of Jesus Christ. Again take a closer look at Romans 16:17,

> I urge you, brothers, to watch out for those who cause divisions and put obstacles in your way that are contrary to the teaching you have learned. Keep away from them!

The warning is not against the difference, but divisiveness!

Fact five: We are *all* erring brethren! We have been taught not to associate with "erring brethren." Brethren, there aren't any other kind. Now there are "false" brethren to be sure! And everyone who differs with us is not necessarily a brother. But every born again brother is one who makes mistakes in both doctrine and life. Those genuinely committed to Christ should be loved and helped; not marked and avoided.

Fact six: The *"real"* problem is a lost world! We've made mountains out of mole hills. The world is going to hell while the church discusses whether we can clap in our assemblies.

The Bible lists these things that keep folks out of heaven:

> Unbelief, rebellion, backsliding, heresy, disobedience, witchcraft, murder, lust, stealing, adultery, abuse, homosexuality, drunkenness, perversion, immorality, swindling, slander, gossip, hatred, divisiveness, greed, envy, strife, deceit, malice, idolatry, lying, backbiting, arrogance, factions, anger, brawling, filthy language, unforgiving spirit, etc.
> (Cf. Rom. 1:18-32, I Cor. 6:9-11, Gal. 5:19-21, Eph. 4:25-32, Col. 3:5-10, II Tim. 3:1-5, Rev. 21:8.)

I see no emphasis on the "honest mistakes" of God-fearing, Bible-believing, Christ-loving baptized believers. Are our differences important? Yes! Must we live by our convictions? Yes! But these things are not in the same class with the lists above. Strong preaching is called for on the former. Patience, tolerance and more study is required on the latter.

## FACING THE TWENTY-FIRST CENTURY!

One hundred years ago (1889) at Sand Creek, Illinois, good brethren formally declared they would no longer regard other children of God with whom they disagreed as brethren. I don't even know what issue split them. But this sad practice has continued to this present day. The result has been the disgraceful splintering and sectarianizing of the body of Christ. We will never win a lost world to Jesus as long as we keep fighting among ourselves. It's time to call a halt to it!

It is December, 1989, as I write this final chapter. We are entering the decade of the 90's. In ten years (if Jesus does not come) we will enter the twenty-first century. That little directory of churches of Christ already lists twenty different kinds of us. I've heard no outcry that "they shouldn't be in the same book with us!" Wouldn't it be wonderful if, by the year 2000, we could add one more code? "IM", perhaps, (for brethren who use instrumental music in worship).

God already has them in His book! And we have a broader base of agreement with them than with some of the others listed in *Where the Saints Meet*. It would at least make the statement that though we have serious disagreement, *we love each other too much to divide!*

## A PRAYER, A PLEA AND A PLAN!

Many will remember A.G. Hobbs' tract by this title! He recalls the prayer of Jesus for unity (John 17:20,21). He cites the plea for unity by Paul (I Cor. 1:10). His plan for unity is the seven ones of Eph. 4:4-6. It was a good tract. It's a good prayer, plan and plea. May I add this to the plan?

1. Preach the word (II Tim. 4:2)! Discover which things are matters of faith, and which are not. Don't compromise truth with anyone!
2. Accept all baptized believers as being in the Family.
3. Don't draw lines of fellowship on opinion matters!

Wouldn't there be celebrating in the streets if the walls of hostility came down between God's children? We could enter the twenty-first century as "One Family." We would still have problems and differences as we helped each other to a better understanding of God's Word and a closer walk with Jesus. But that oneness, Jesus said, would bring a lost world to believe He was the Son of God.

Jesus thought the unity of believers was worth dying for. Do you think it might be worth living for? Let's stop the fighting! Let's start uniting! Let's get together!

*Don't shoot: we may both be on the same side!*